This Book

Belongs to :

Hi!
We are happy to share with you this book to learn how to write and
Read and of course you'll definitely do it.

And please if you like this book, ask you mom or dad to help you write a review
on Amazon!

This review make me happy and encourage me to make more books like this.

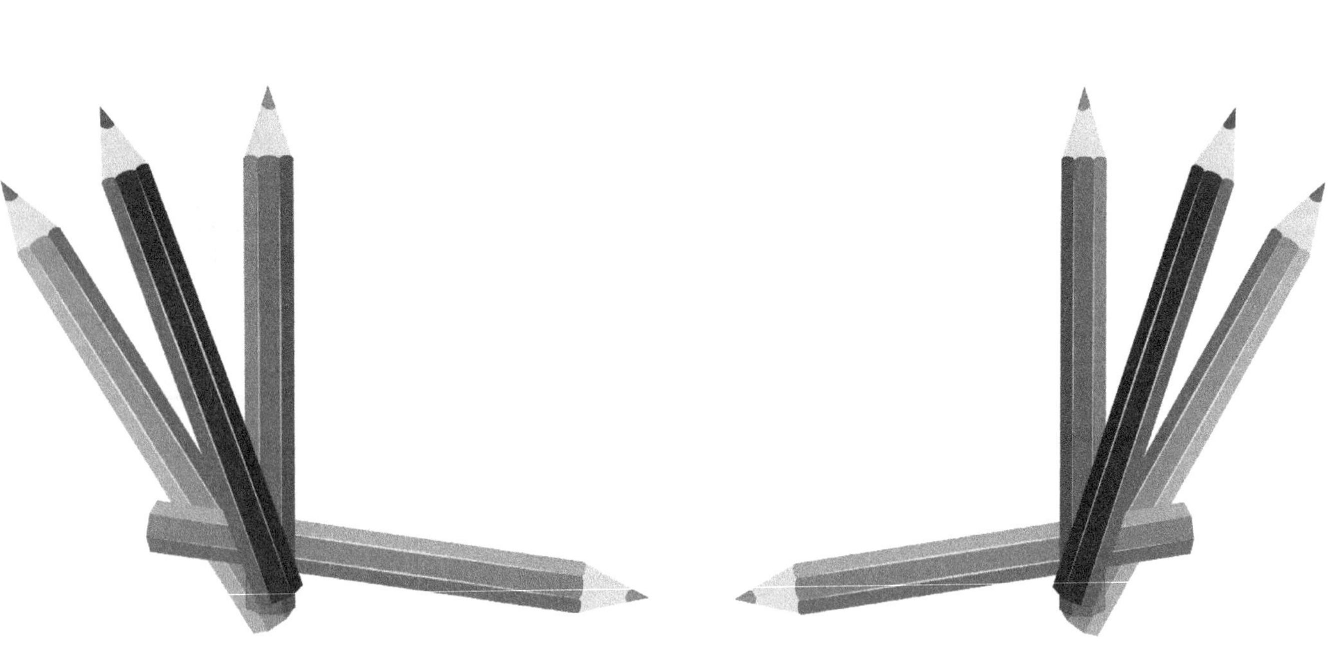

NOTE TO PARENTS :

By age three, your children are
already able to go to school and
learn how to
write and read!
so you have to encourage and help
them step by step for learning,
and of course don't get angry or
scream on them, please.
And even if your children could not
do the right things you have
to encourage them more and never
give up.

Trace with them this lines,numbers,
then letters and words!!

Trace Letters for Toddlers
Ages 3+

First HarperOne hardcover published 2021.

FIRST EDITION

Part 1

Color the Big Numbers

& Trace Numbers

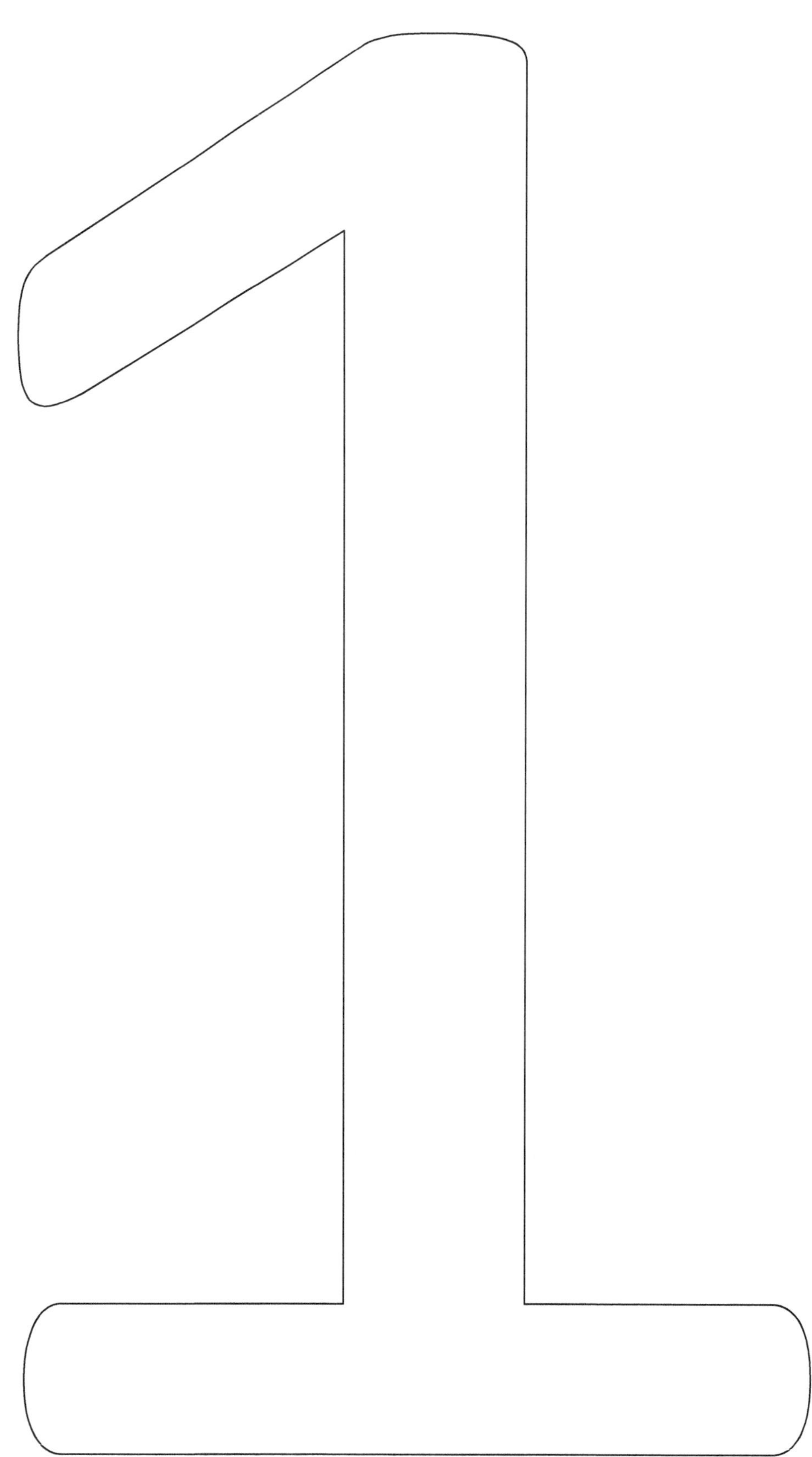

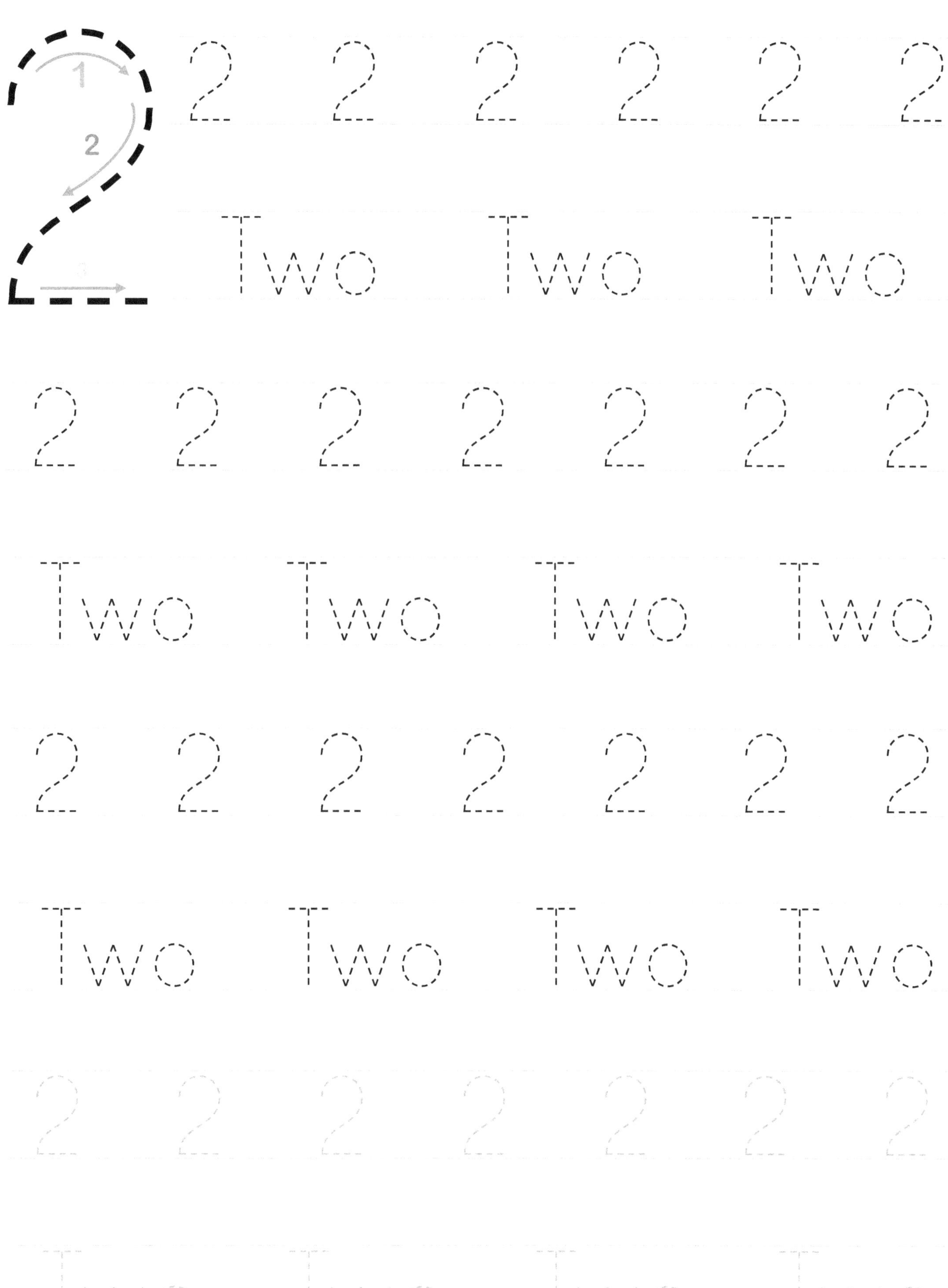

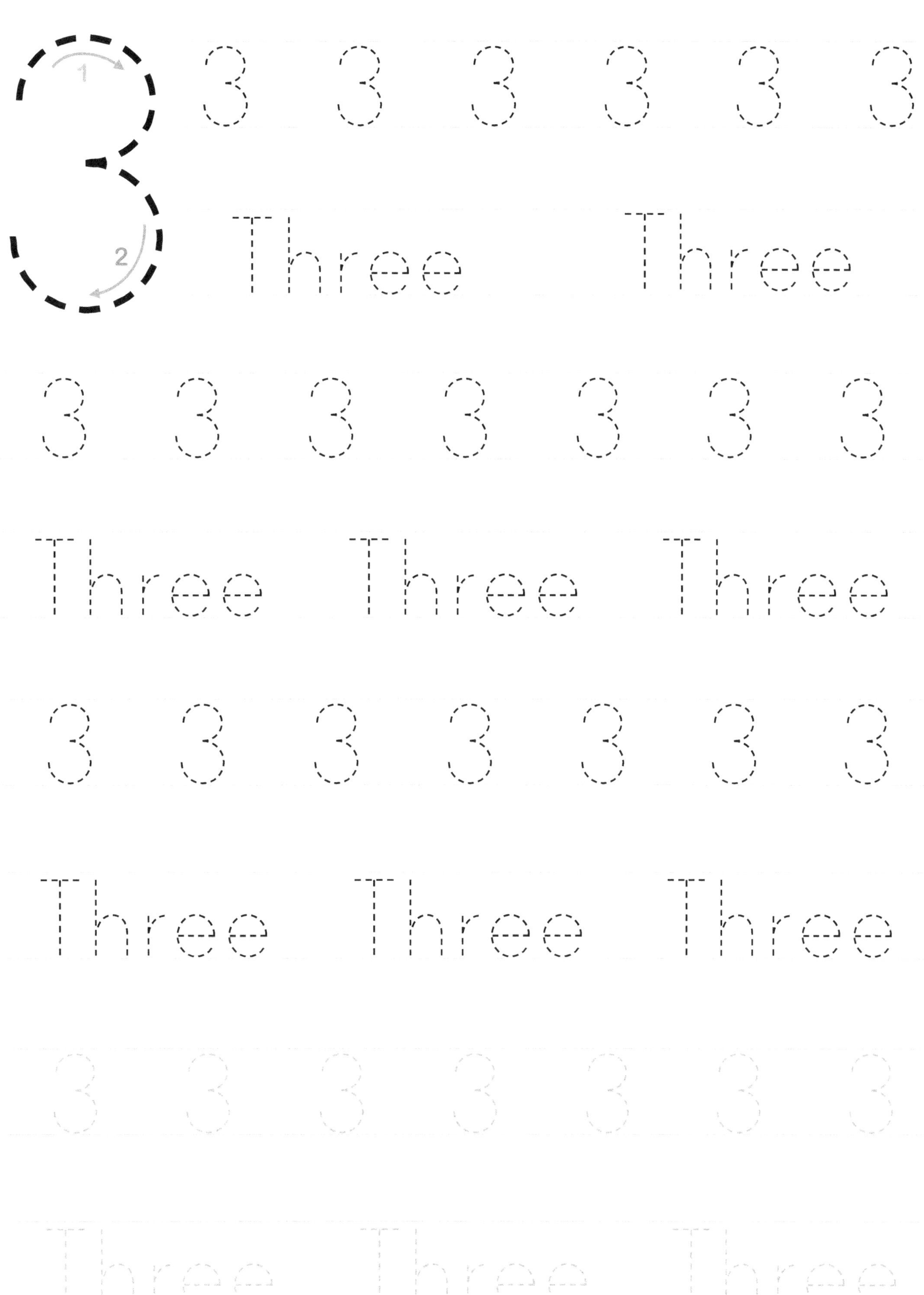

1
2
3 3 3 3 3 3
Three Three
3 3 3 3 3 3 3
Three Three Three
3 3 3 3 3 3 3
Three Three Three
3 3 3 3 3 3 3
Three Three Three

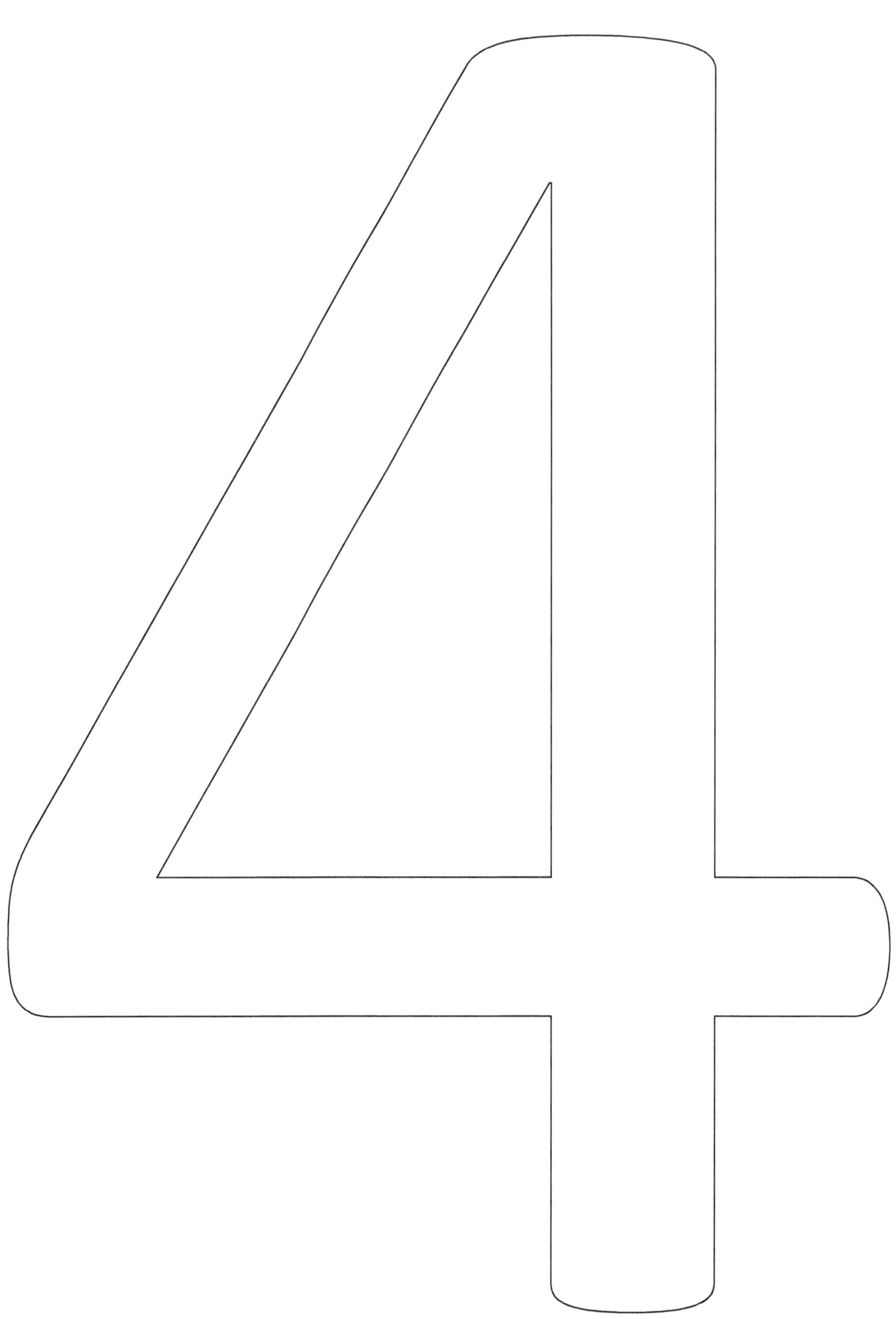

4 4 4 4 4 4 4

1 3 2 4

Four Four Four

4 4 4 4 4 4 4 4

Four Four Four Four

4 4 4 4 4 4 4 4

Four Four Four Four

4 4 4 4 4 4 4 4

Four Four Four Four

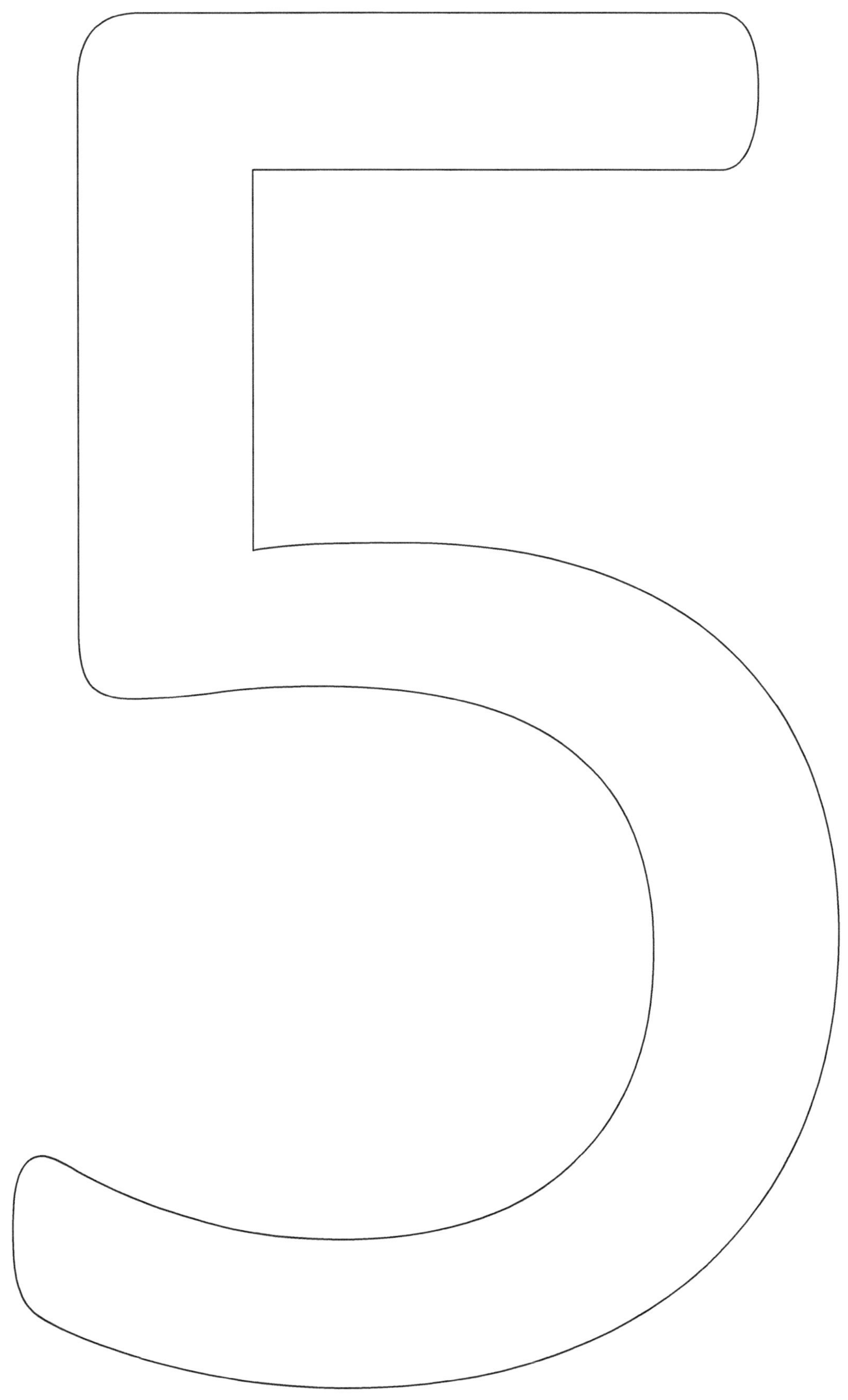

5 5 5 5 5
Five Five Five
5 5 5 5 5 5
Five Five Five Five
5 5 5 5 5 5
Five Five Five Five
5 5 5 5 5 5
Five Five Five Five

6
1
2
3
6 6 6 6 6
Six Six Six
6 6 6 6 6 6
Six Six Six Six
6 6 6 6 6 6
Six Six Six Six
6 6 6 6 6 6
Six Six Six Six

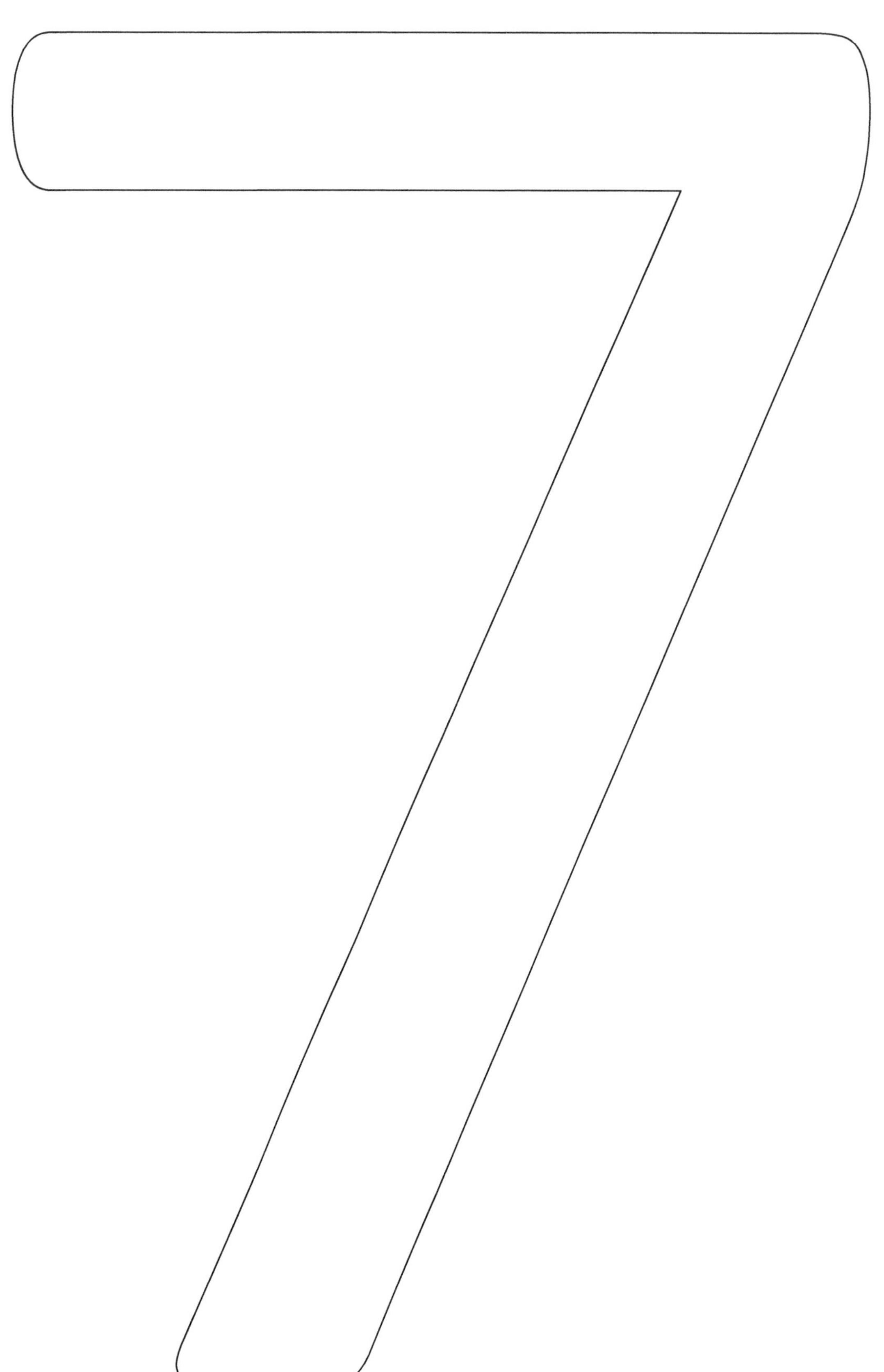

7

1

2

7 7 7 7 7 7

Seven Seven

7 7 7 7 7 7 7

Seven Seven Seven

7 7 7 7 7 7 7

Seven Seven Seven

7 7 7 7 7 7 7

Seven Seven Seven

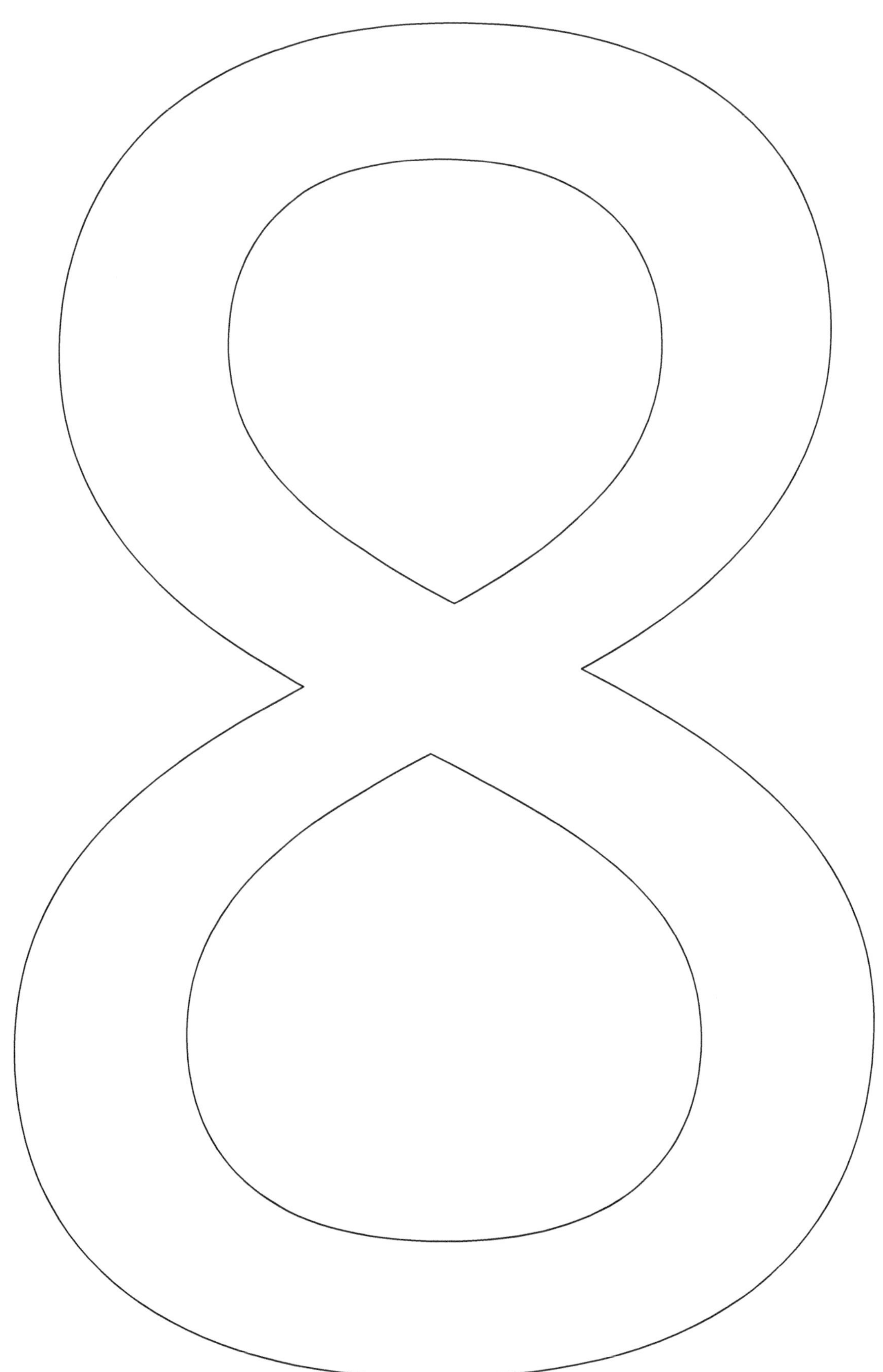

8 8 8 8 8 8 8

1 2 3 4 5 6

Eight Eight

8 8 8 8 8 8 8

Eight Eight Eight

8 8 8 8 8 8 8

Eight Eight Eight

8 8 8 8 8 8 8

Eight Eight Eight

9
2
1
3
9 9 9 9 9 9
Nine Nine Nine
9 9 9 9 9 9 9
Nine Nine Nine Nine
9 9 9 9 9 9 9
Nine Nine Nine Nine
9 9 9 9 9 9 9
Nine Nine Nine Nine

Part 2

Trace Lines

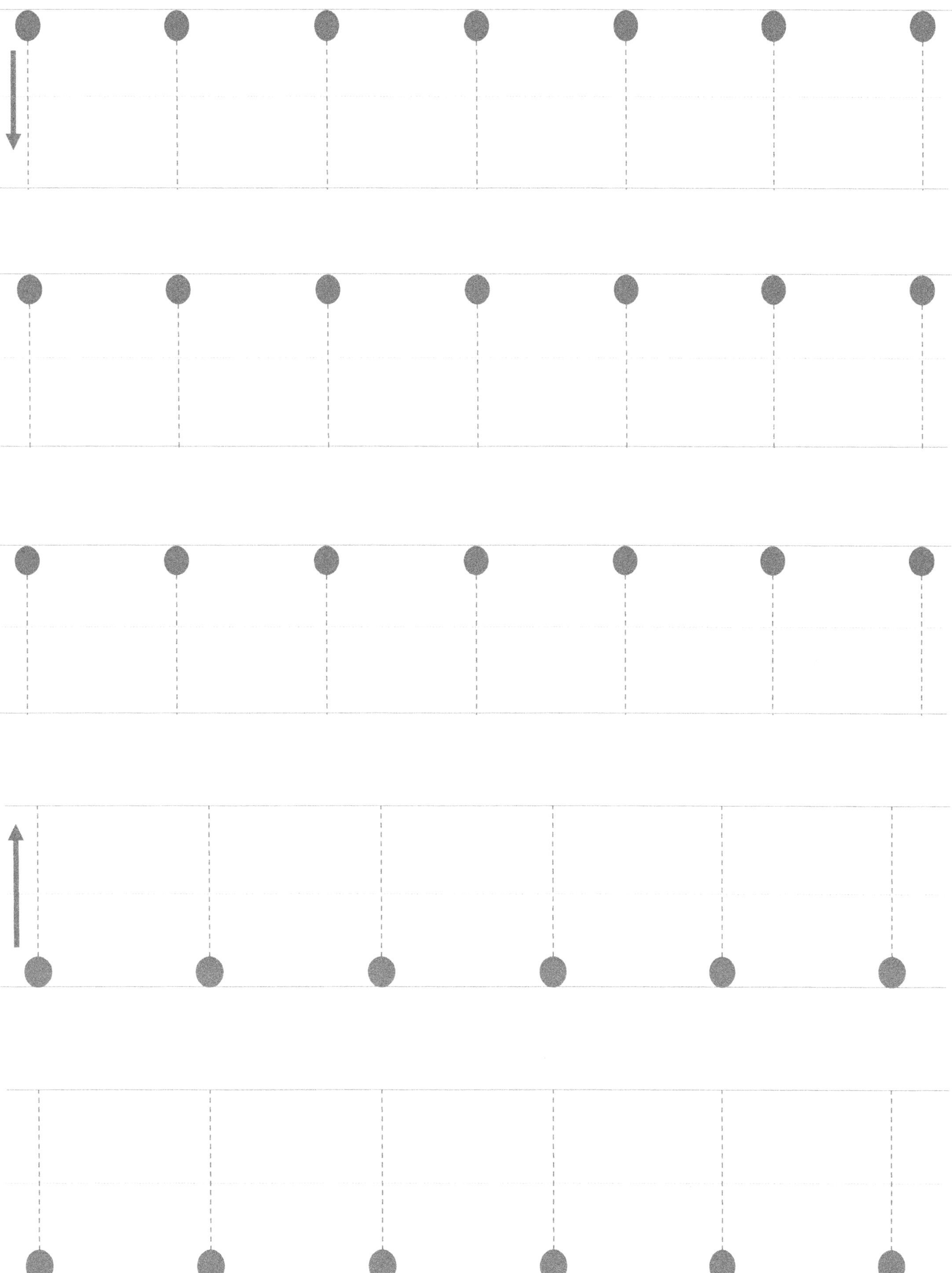

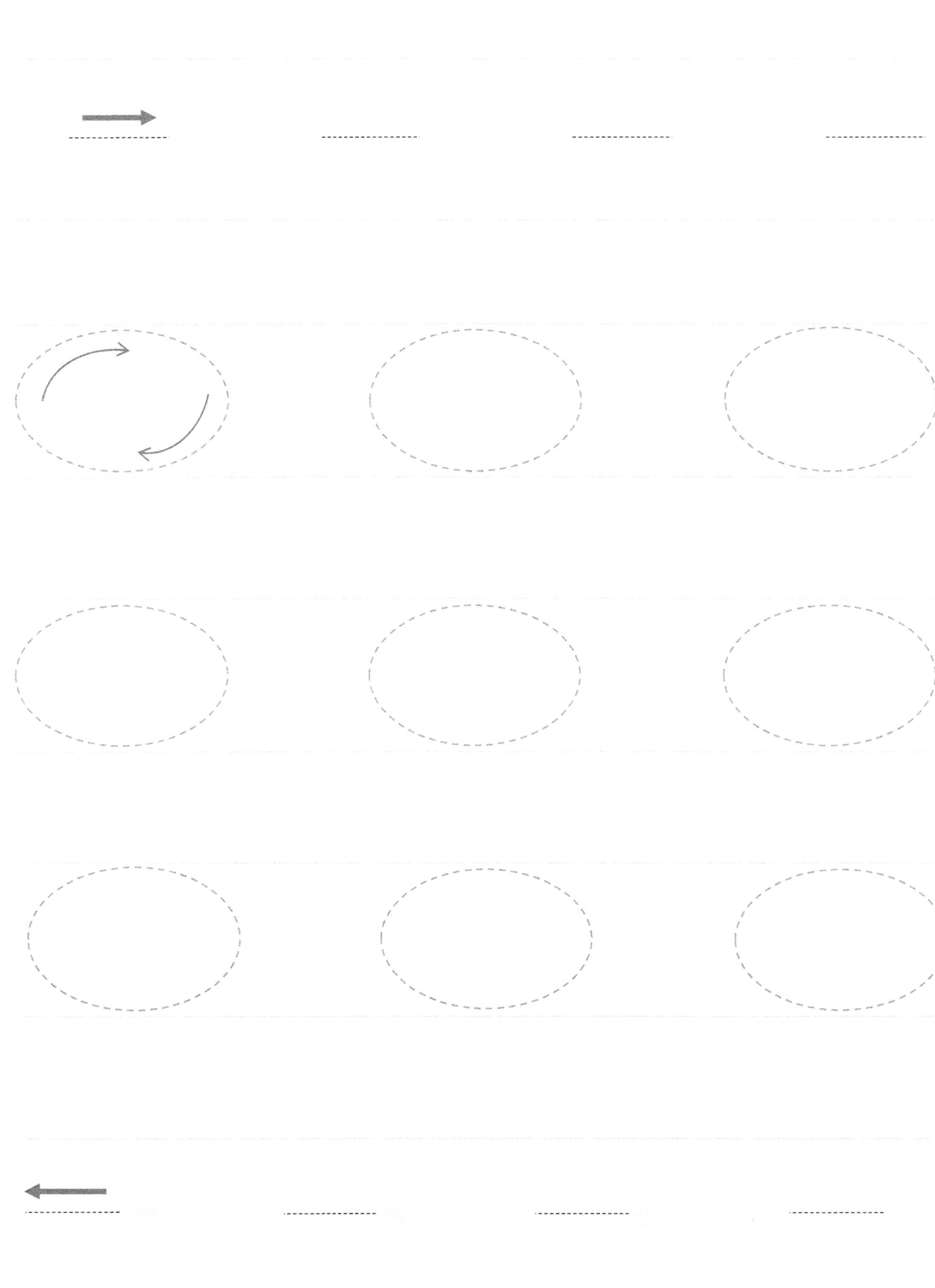

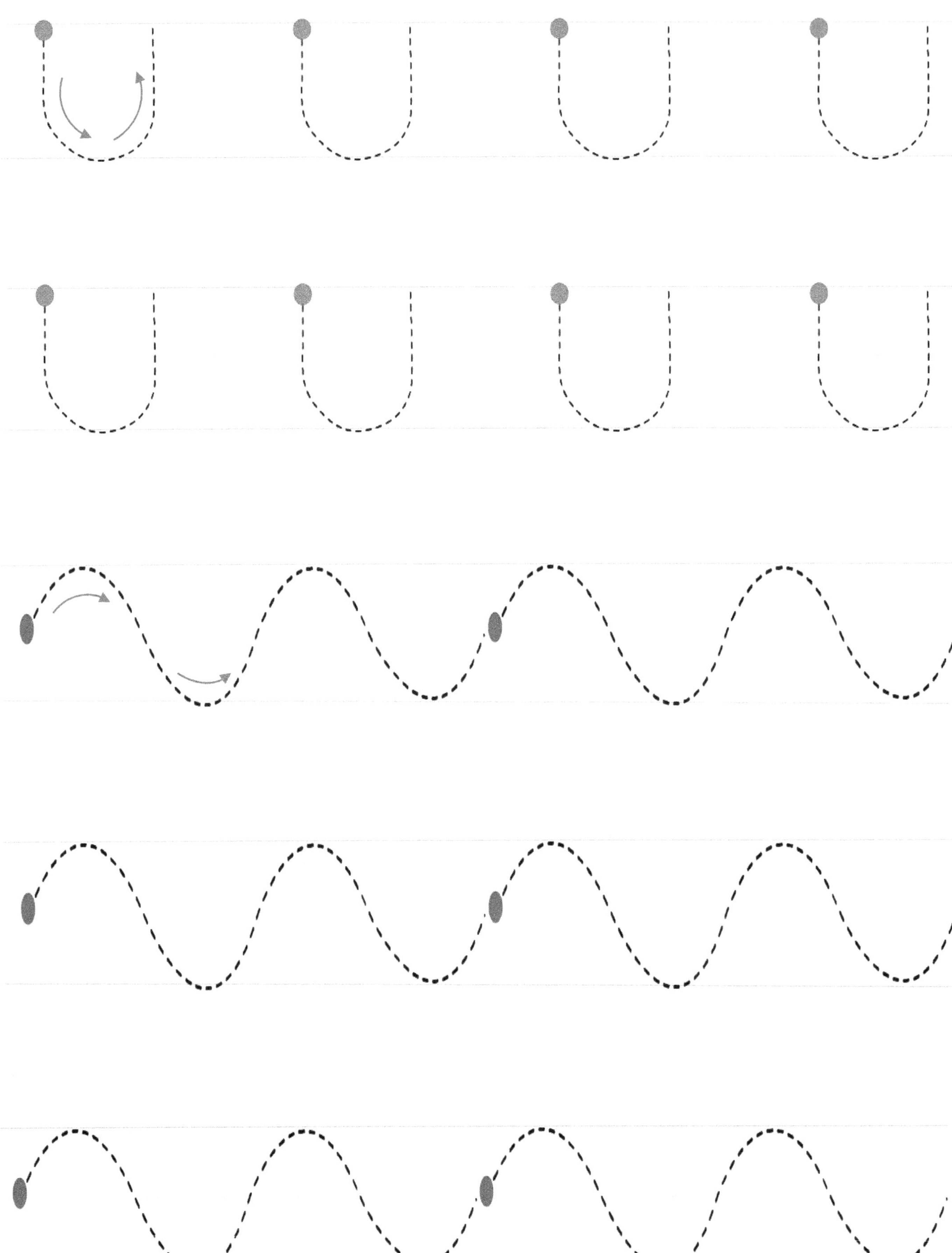

Part 3

Trace Letters

1
2
3

1
2
3

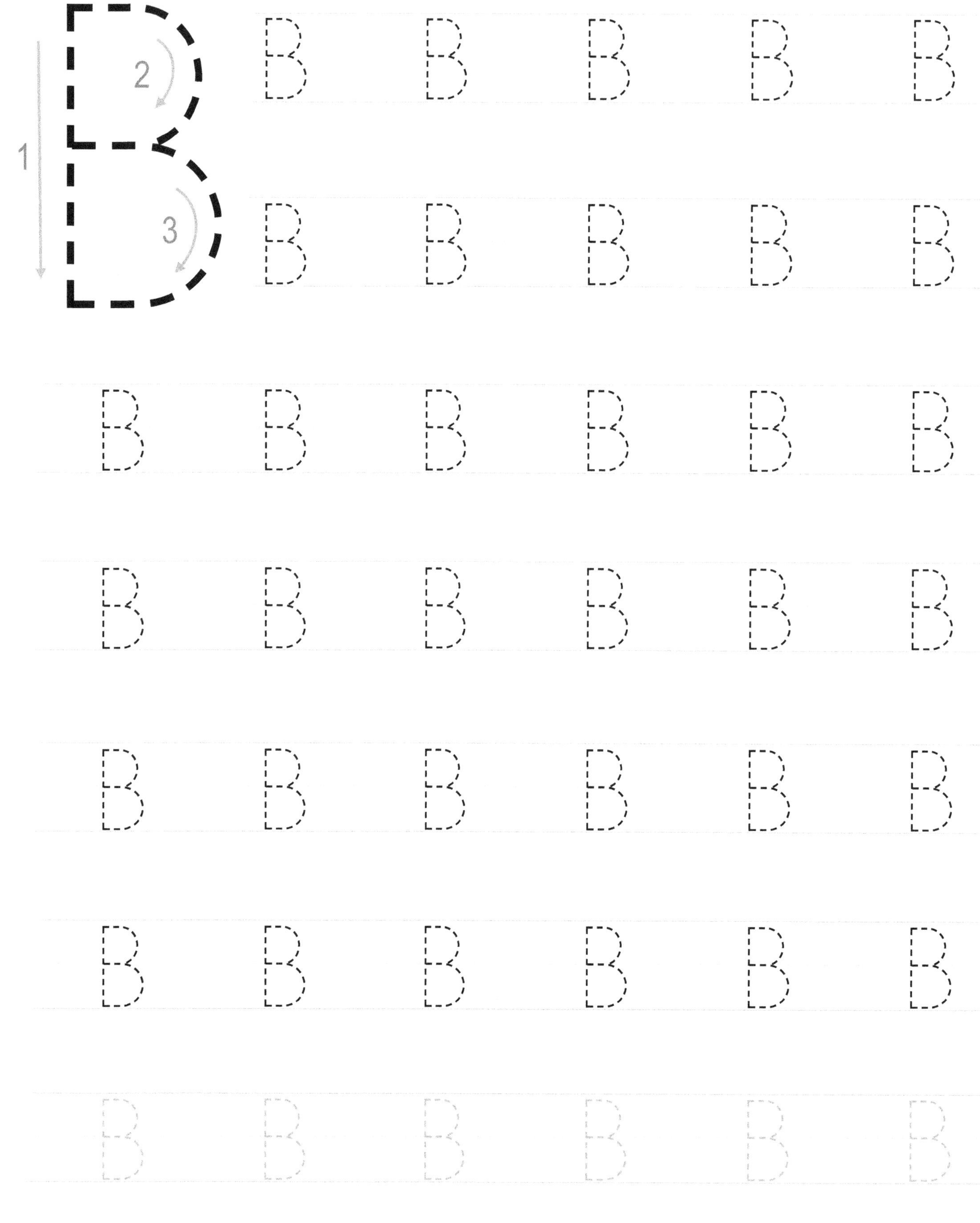

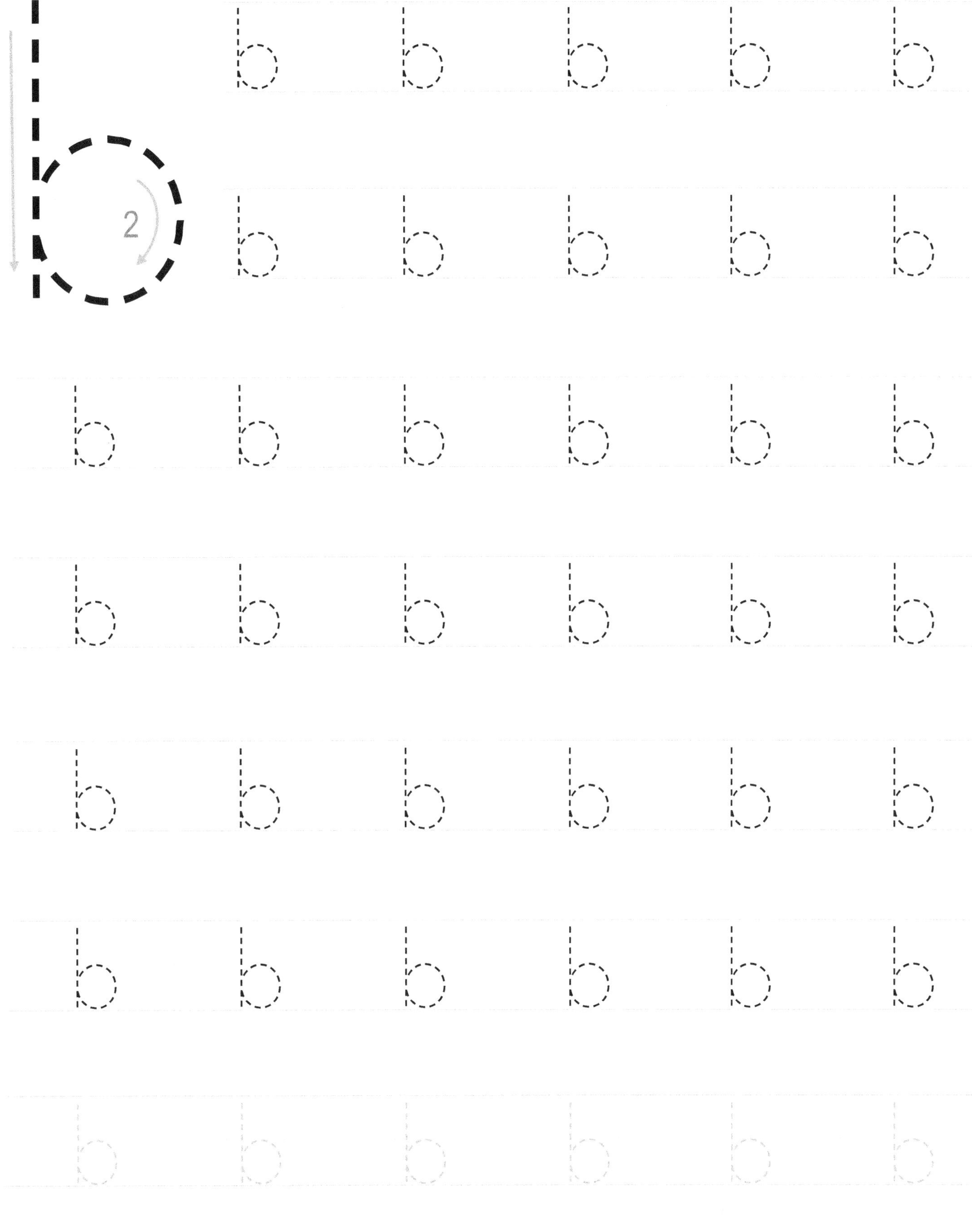

1
2

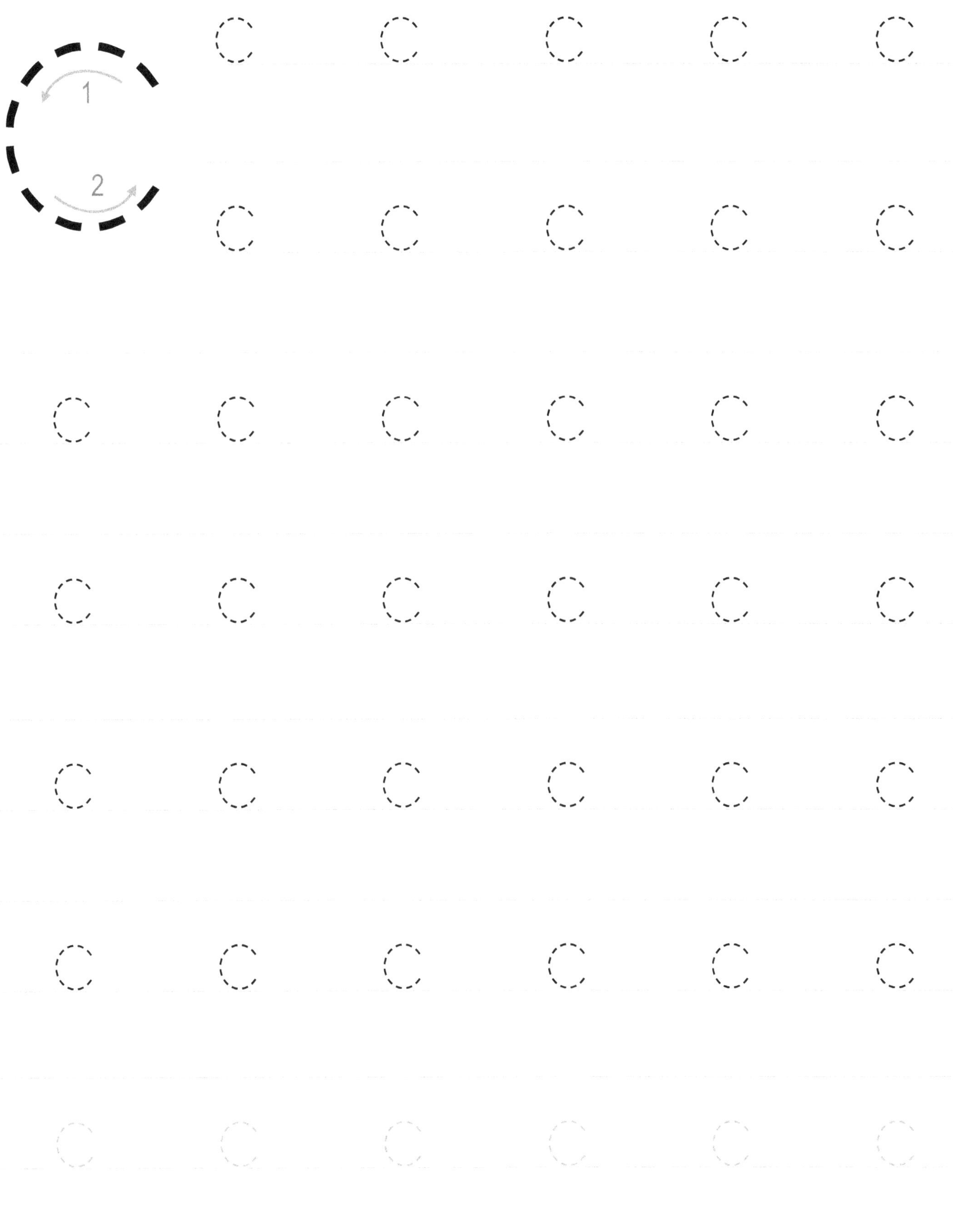
1
2

1
2
3

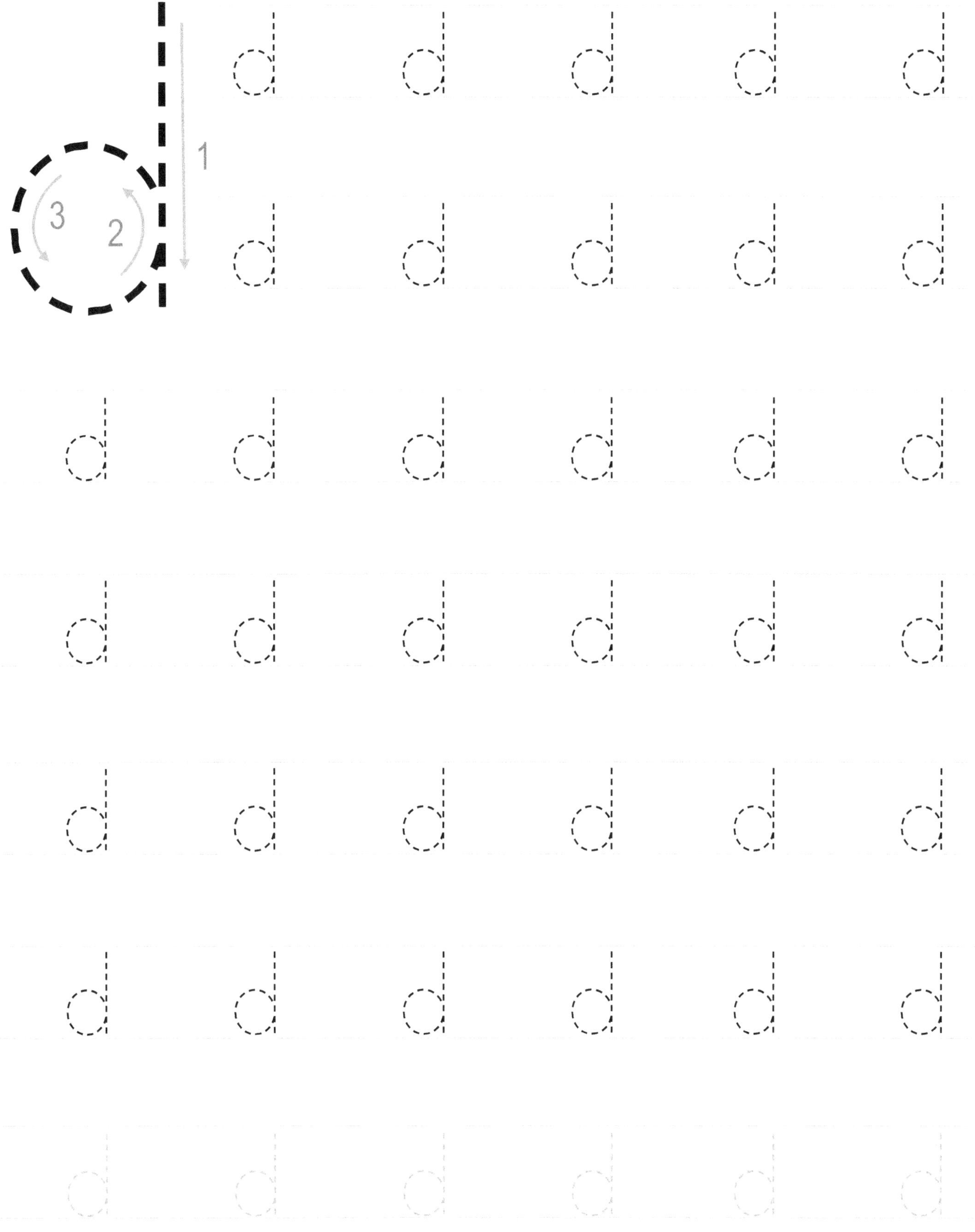
1
3
2

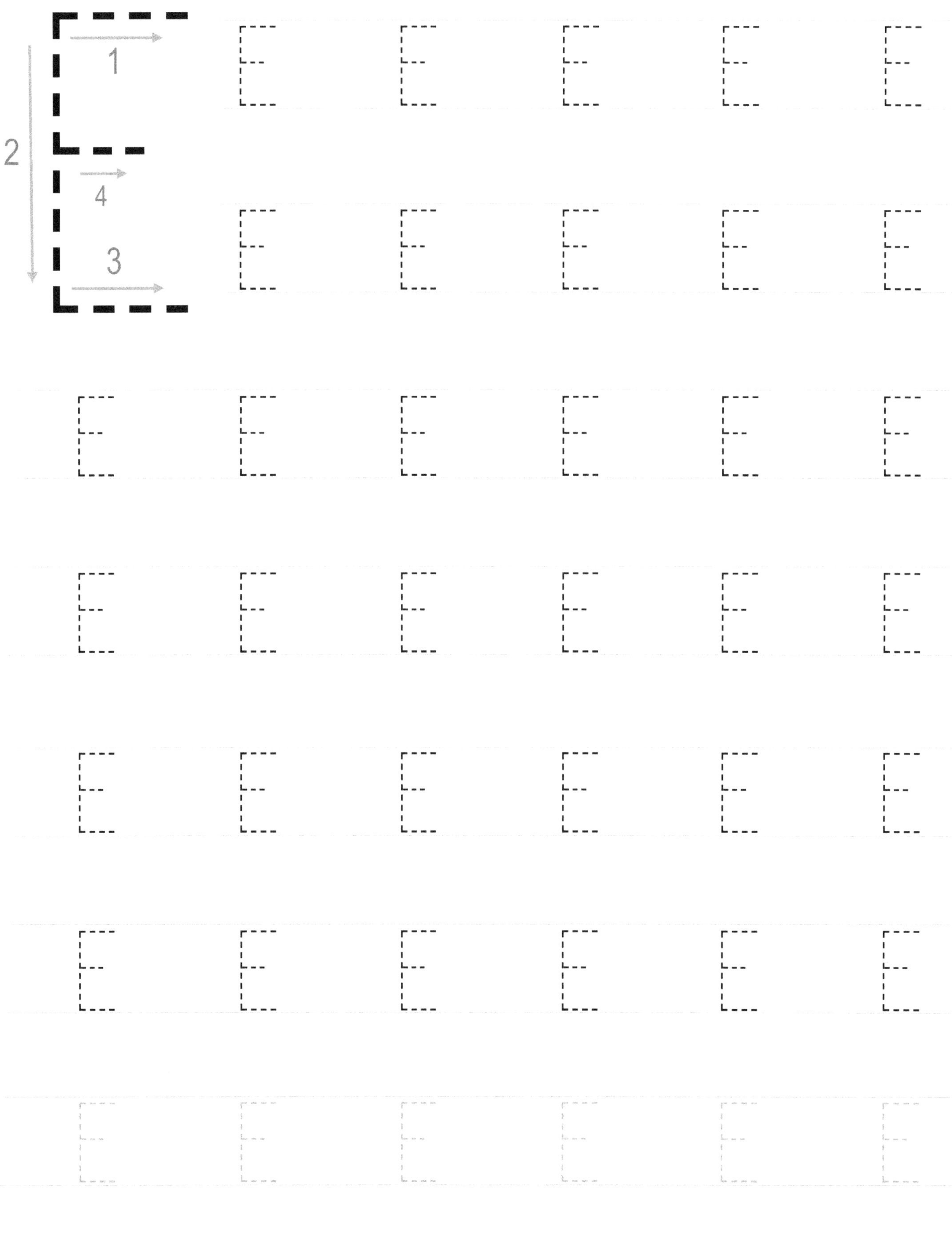
1
2
4
3

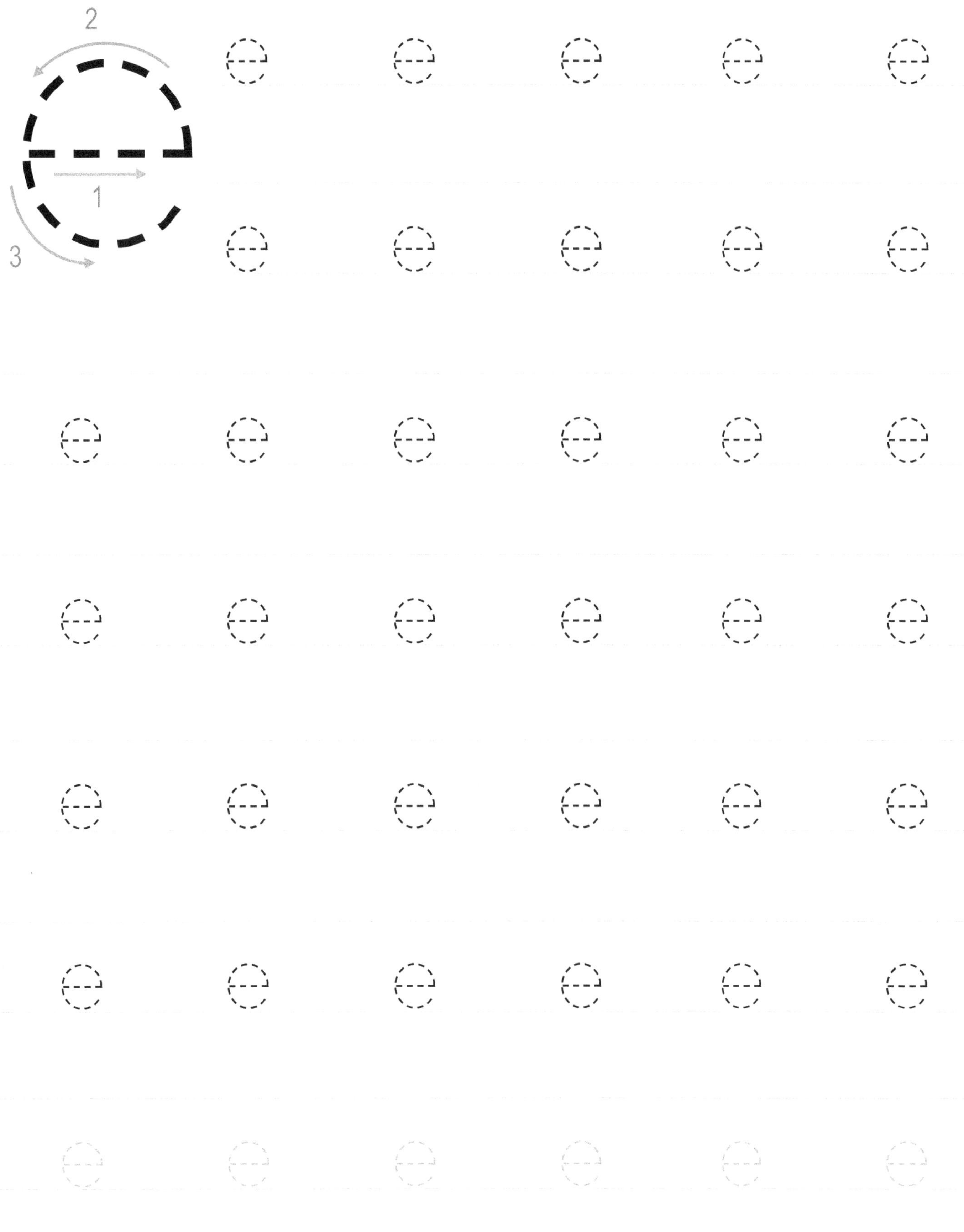
2
1
3

1
2
3

1
2
3

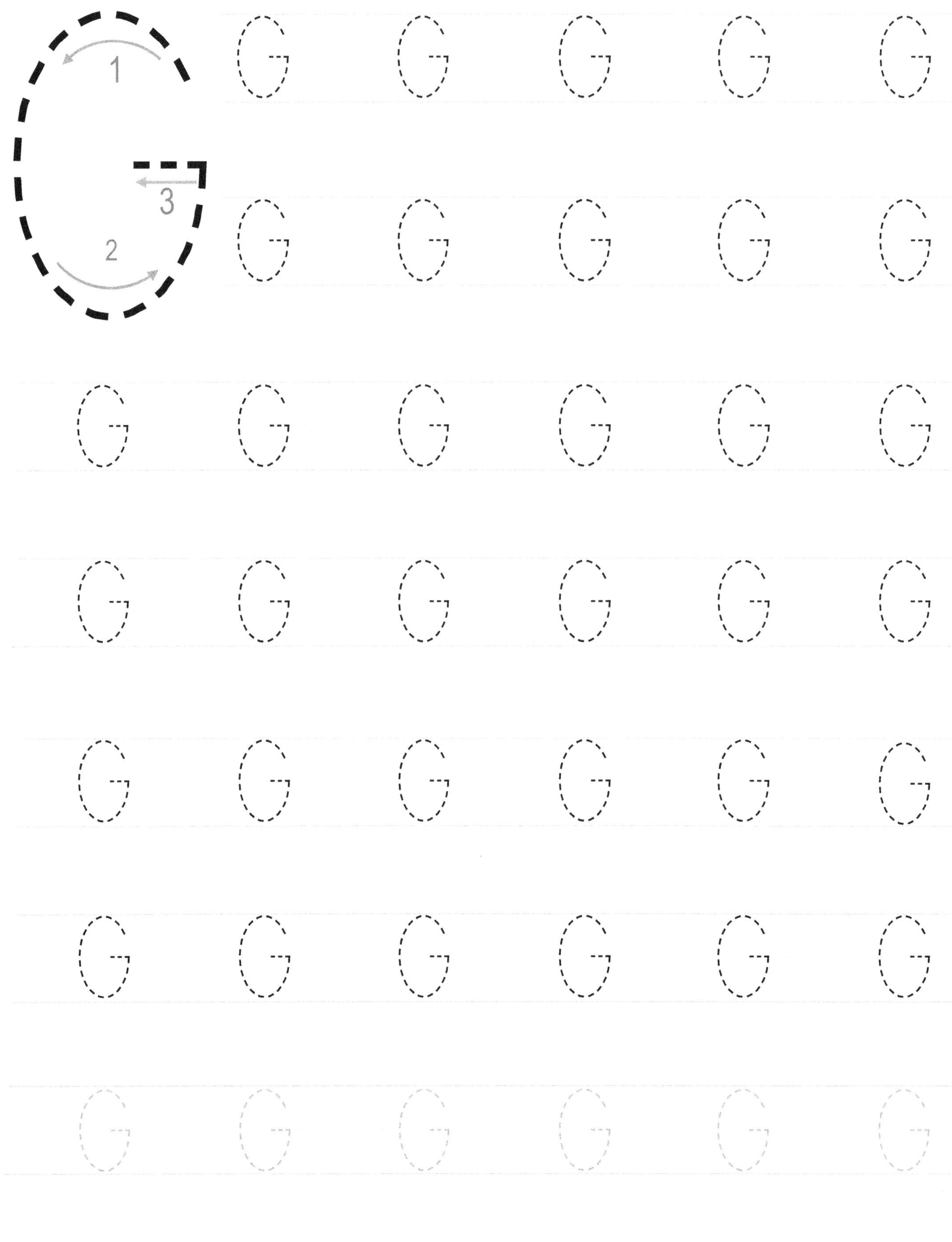
1
3
2

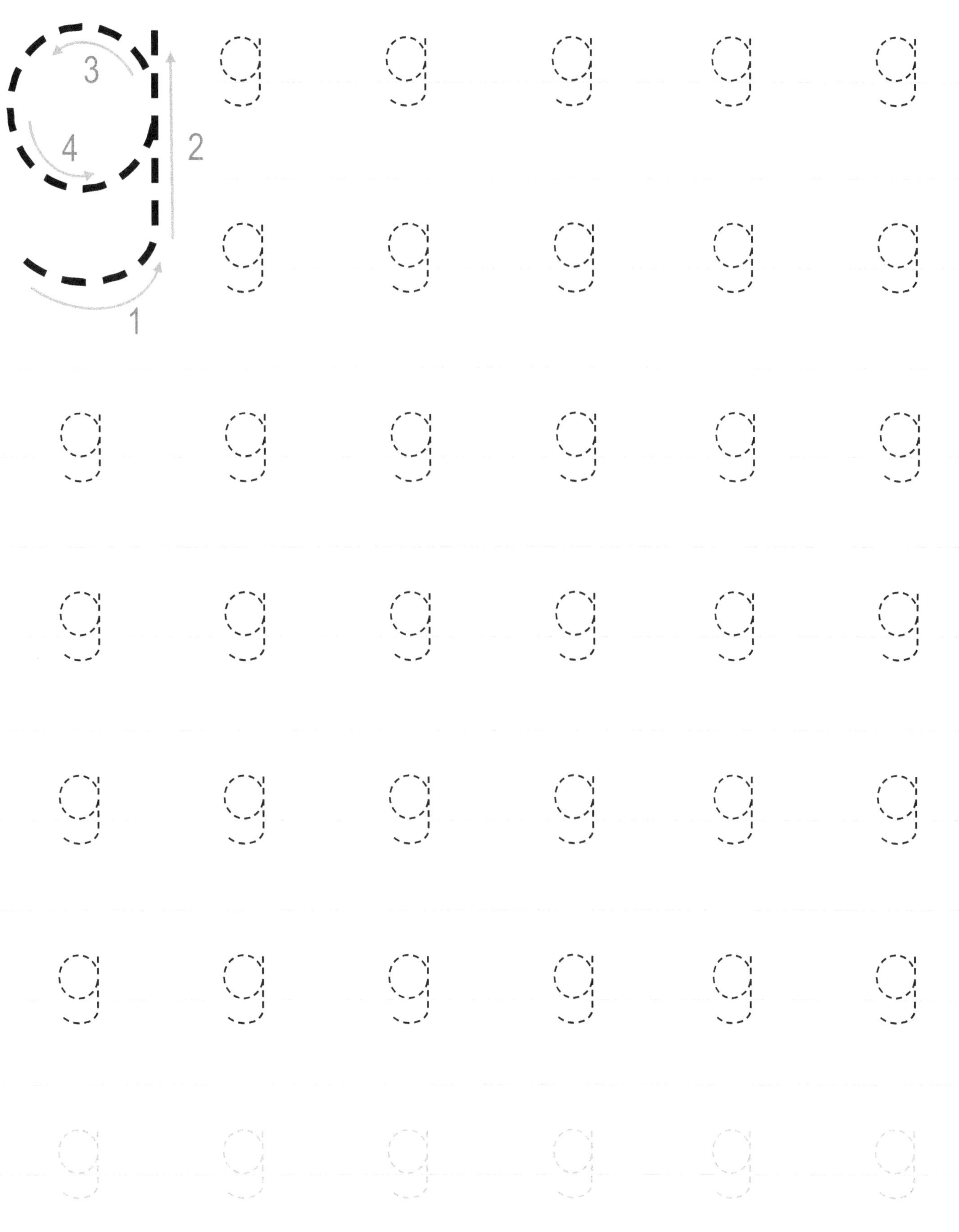
3
4
2
1

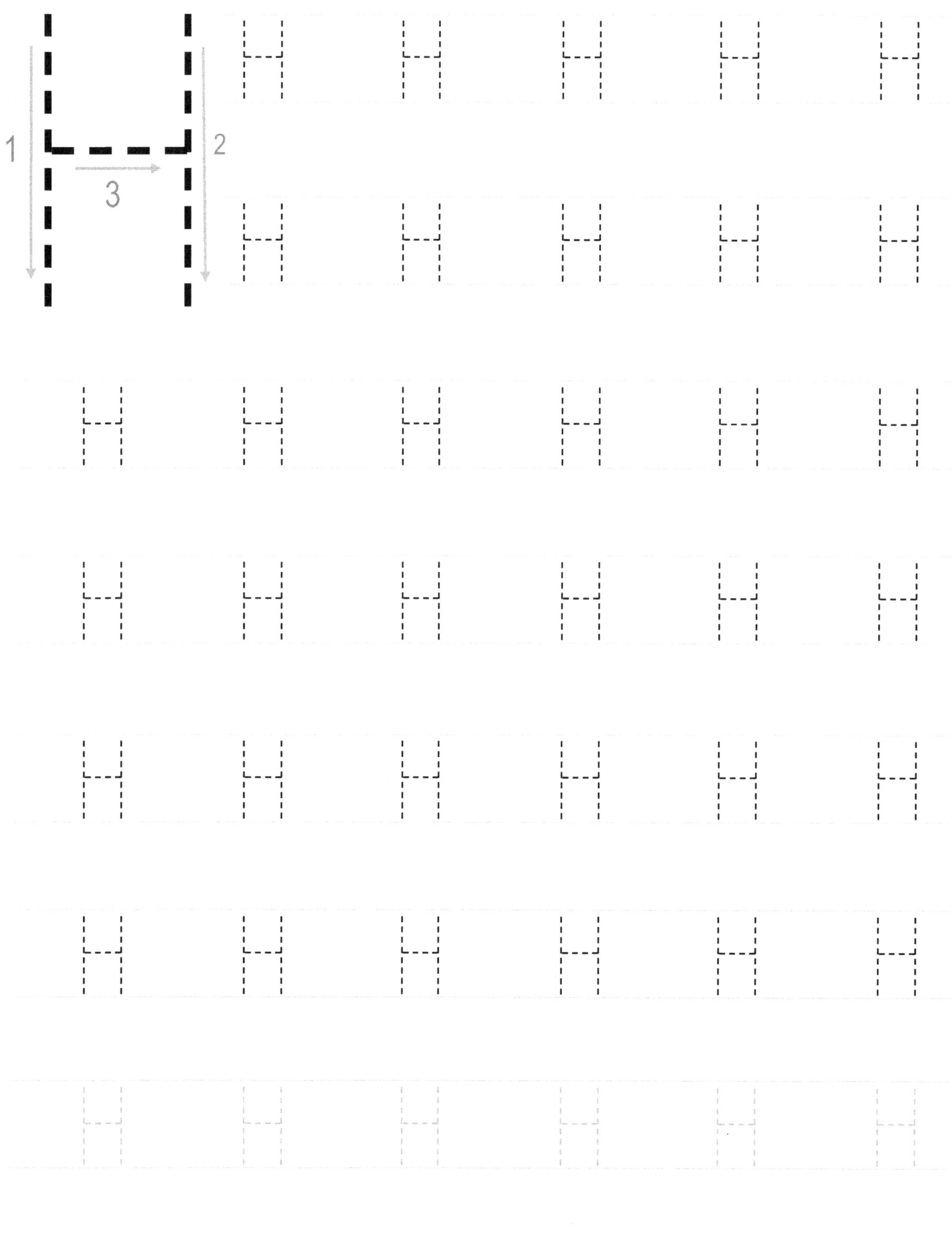
1
2
3

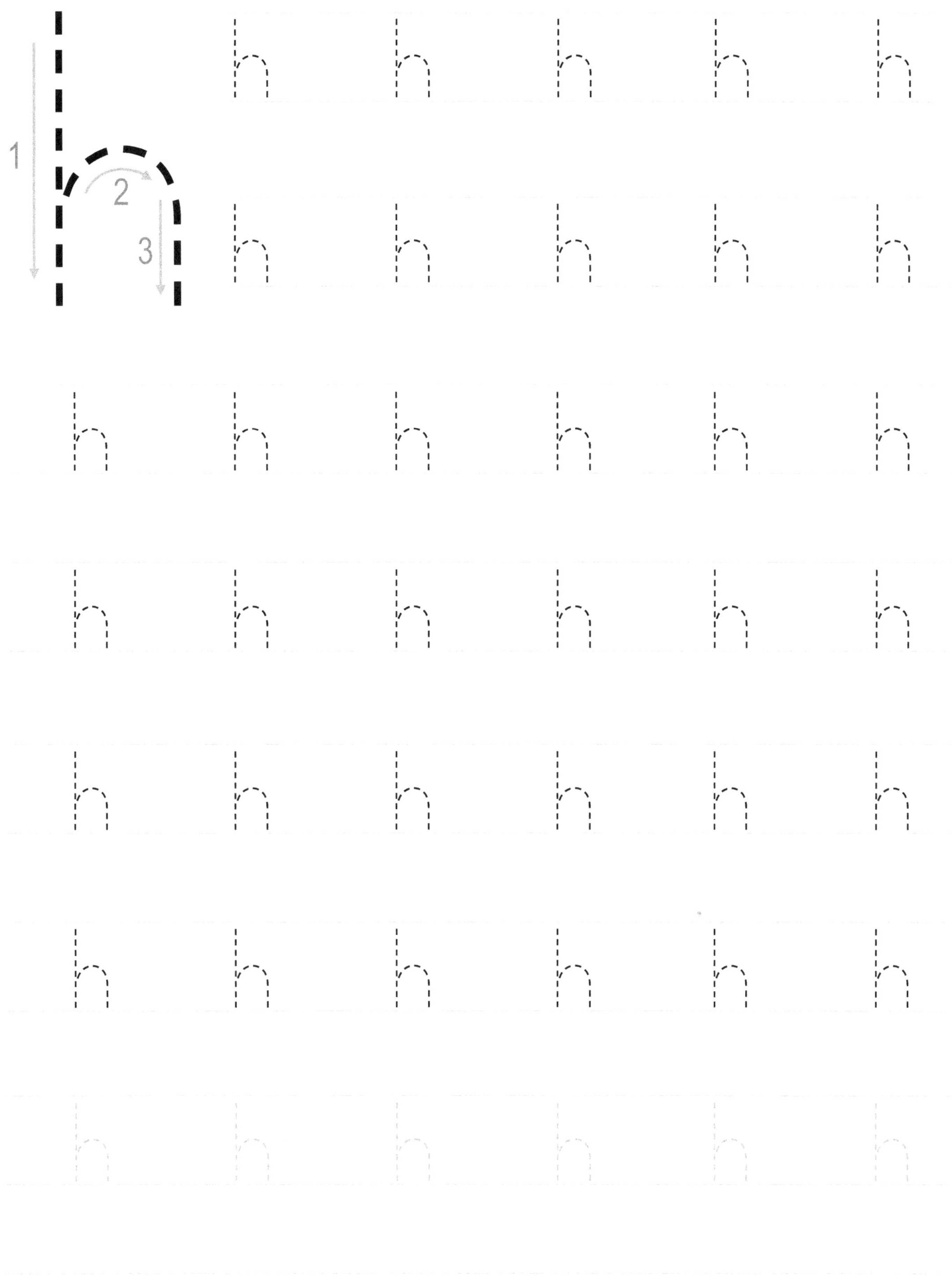
1
2
3

1
2
3

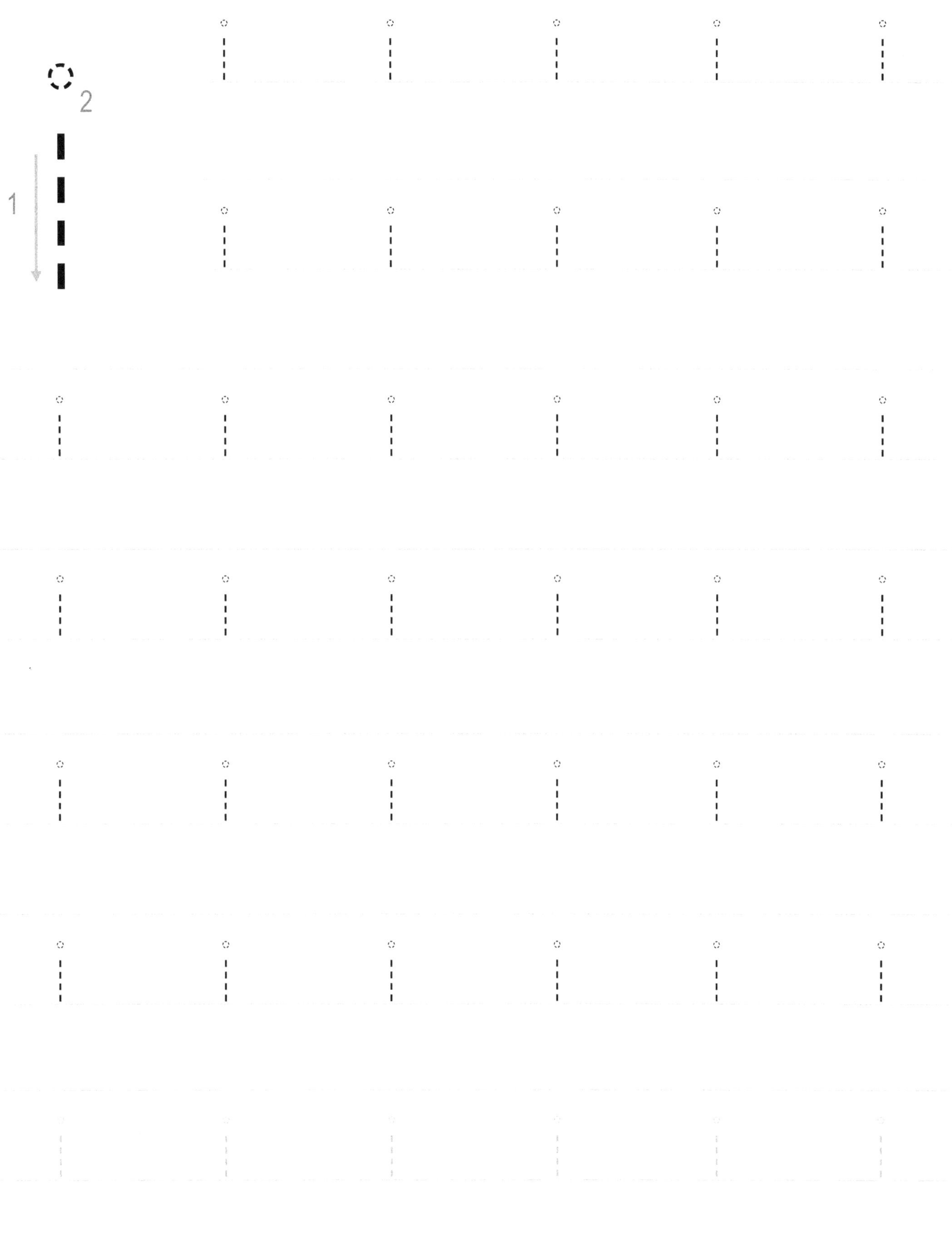
2
1

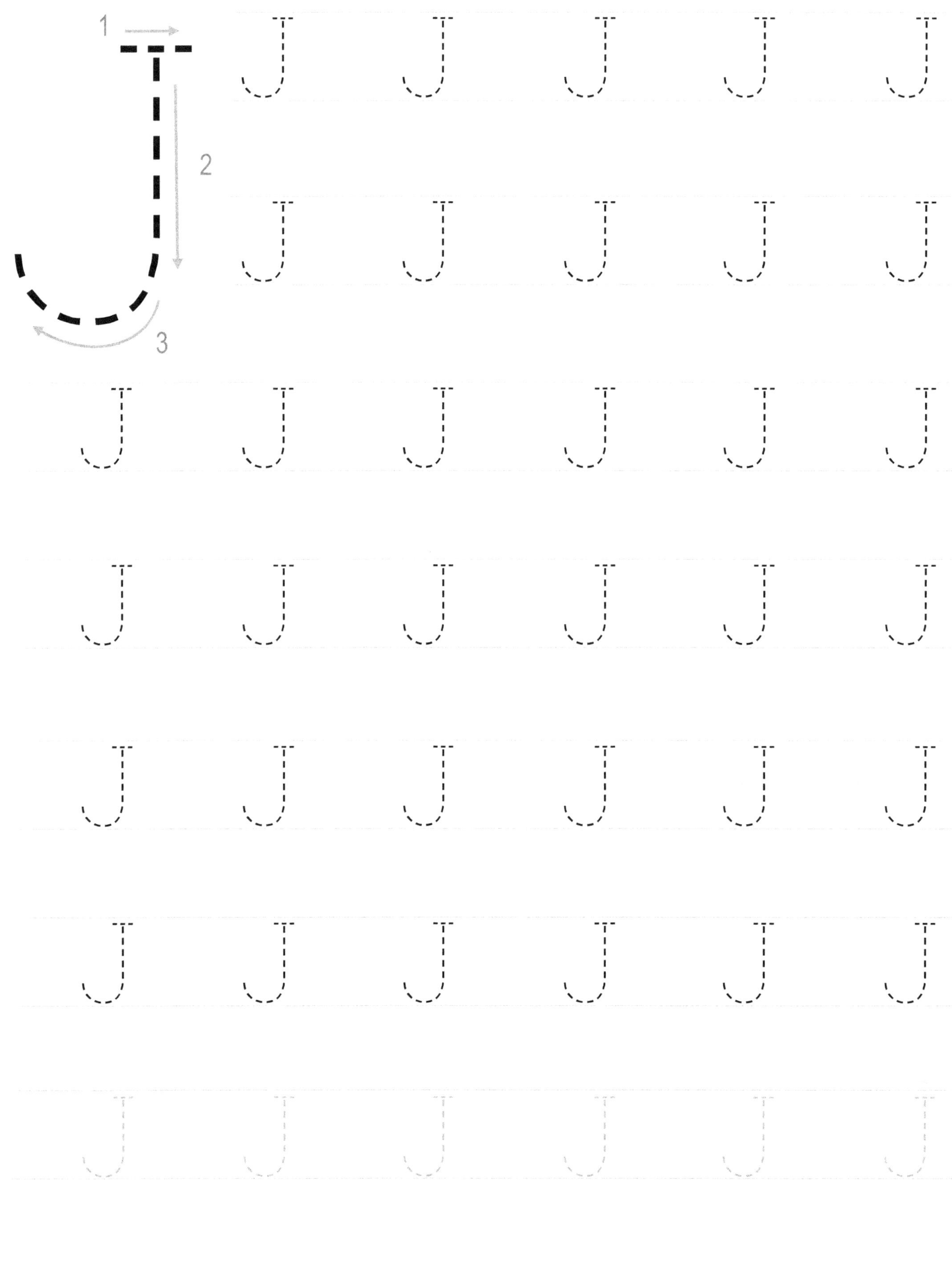
1
2
3

2
1

1
2
3

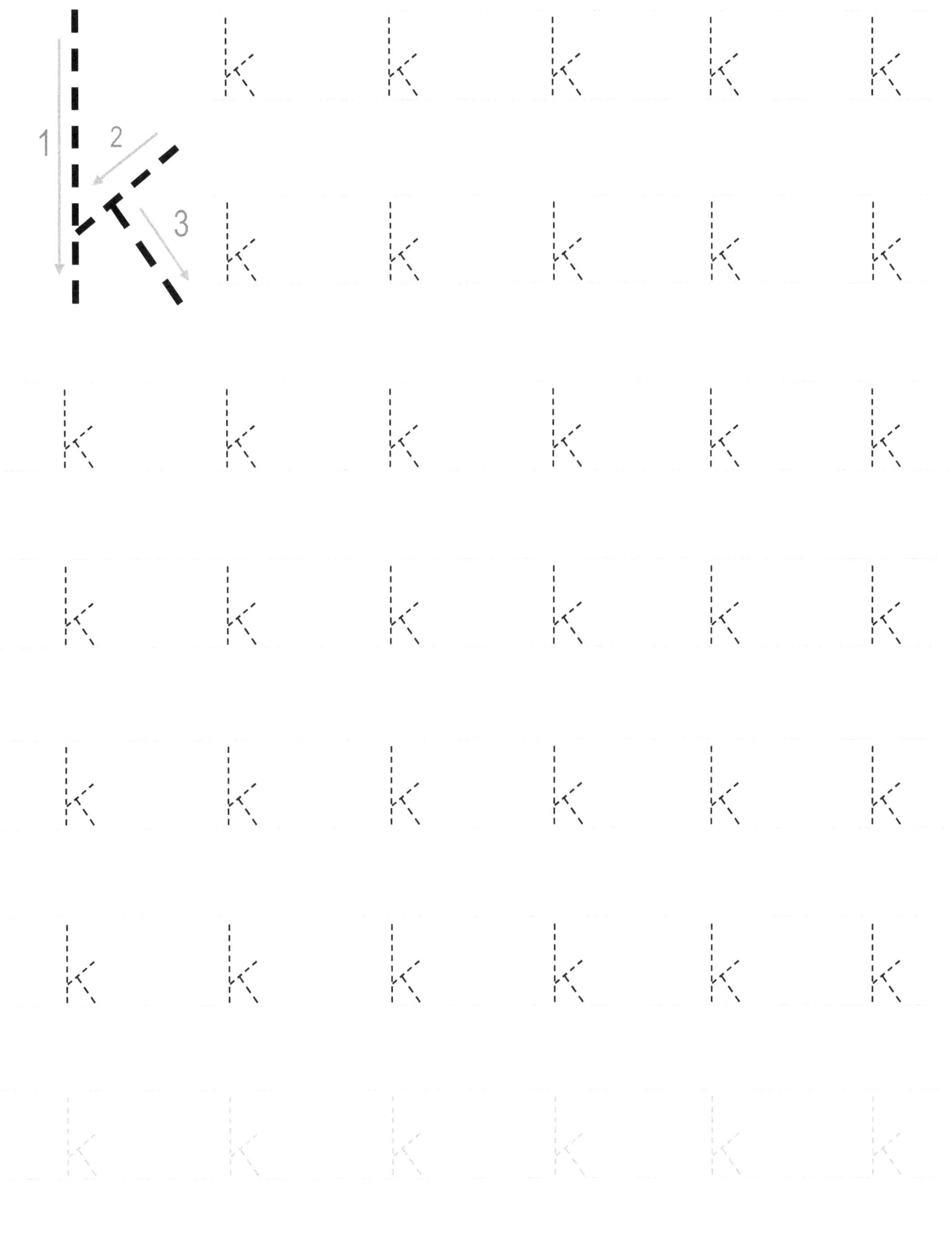
1
2
3

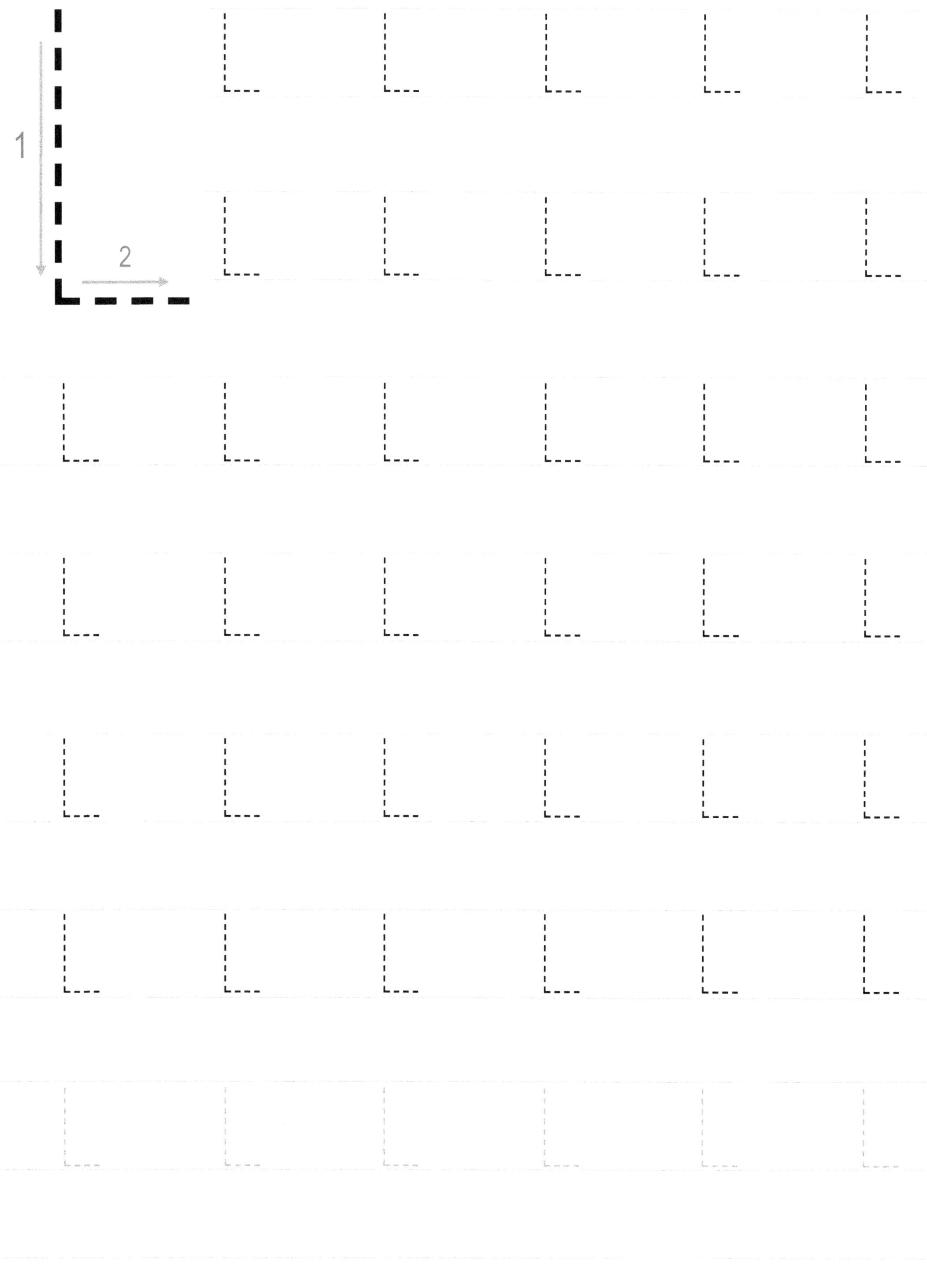
1
2

1

1
2
3
4

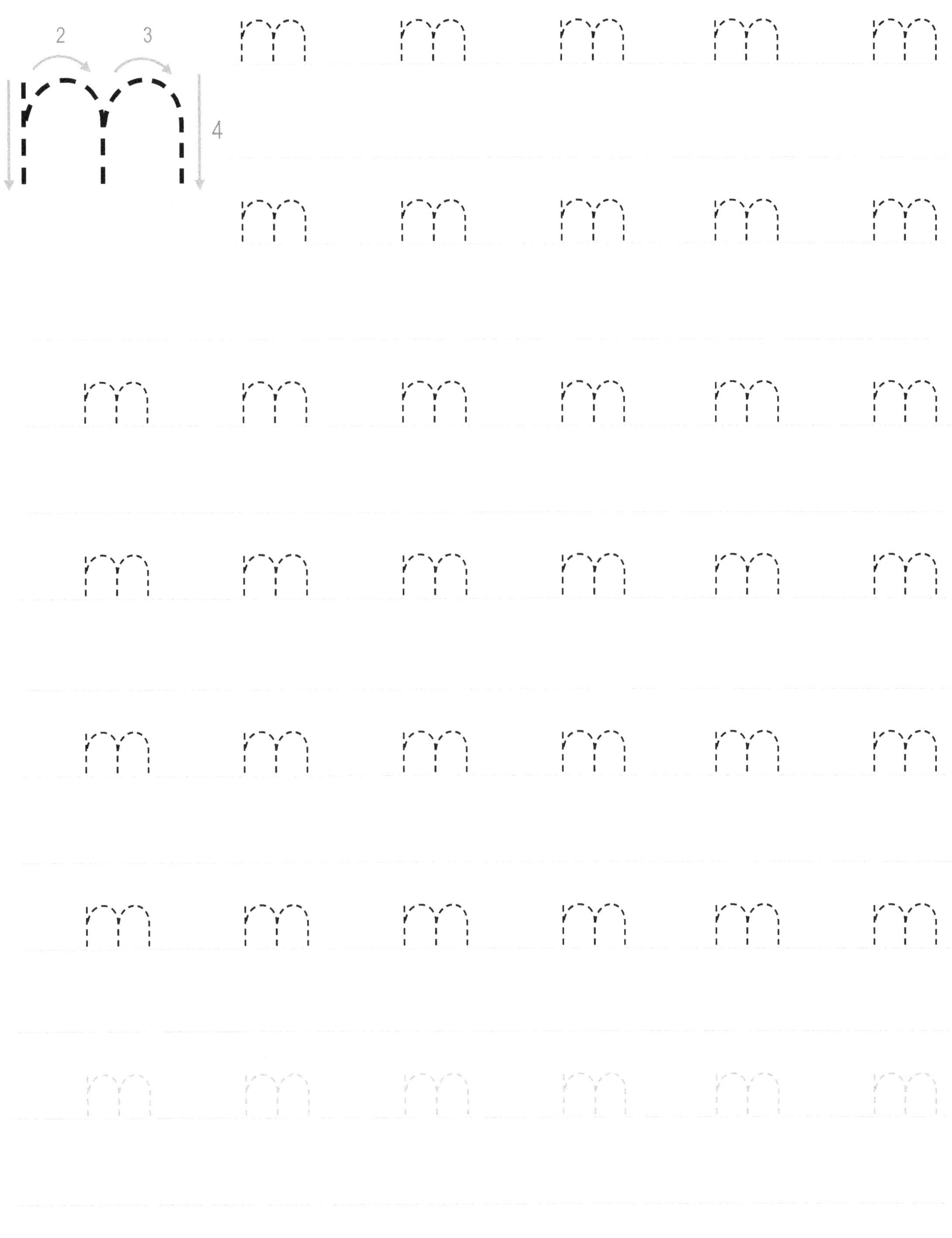

1
2
3
4

1
2
3

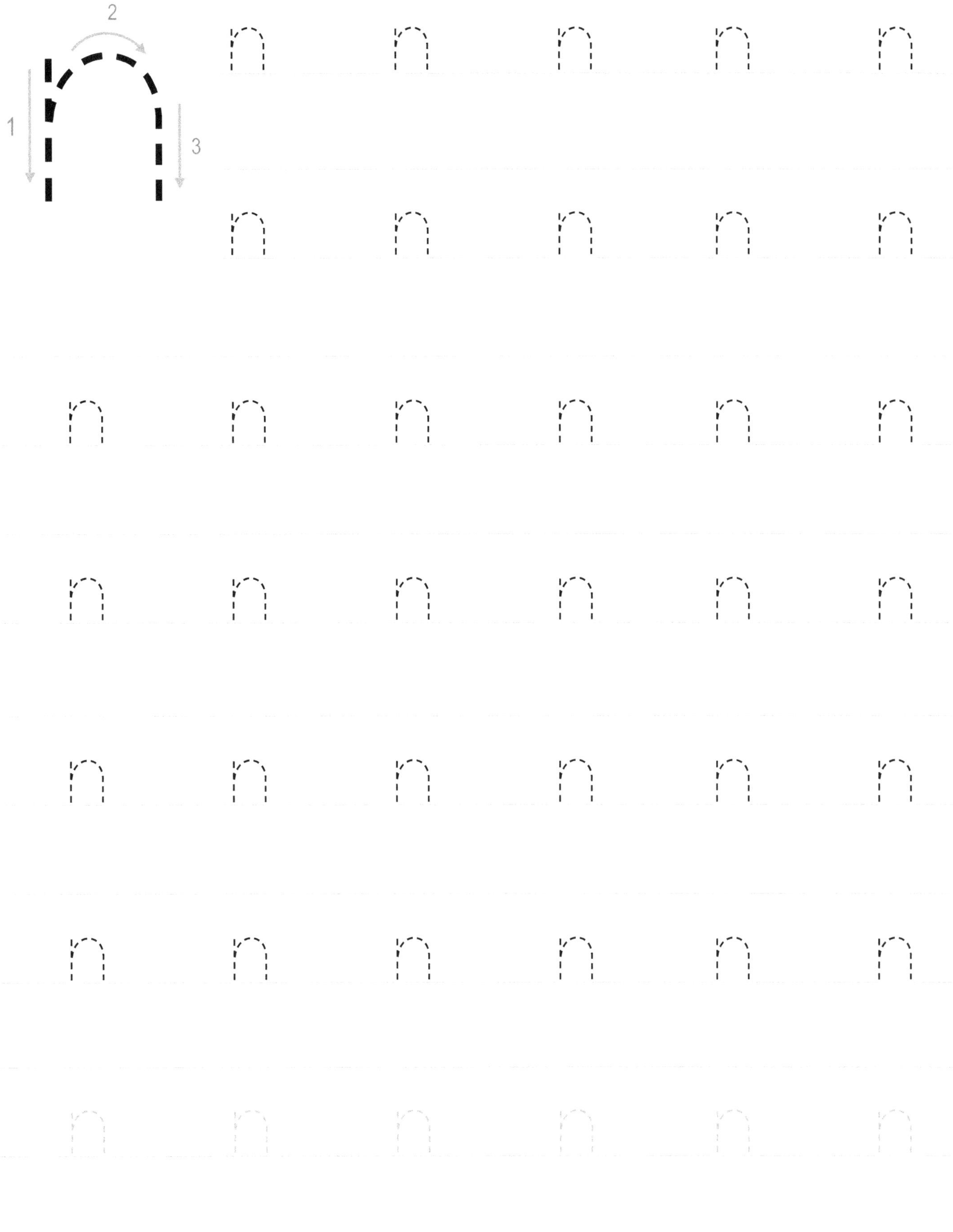
2
1
3
n n n n n
n n n n n
n n n n n n
n n n n n n
n n n n n n
n n n n n n
n n n n n n

1
2
4
3

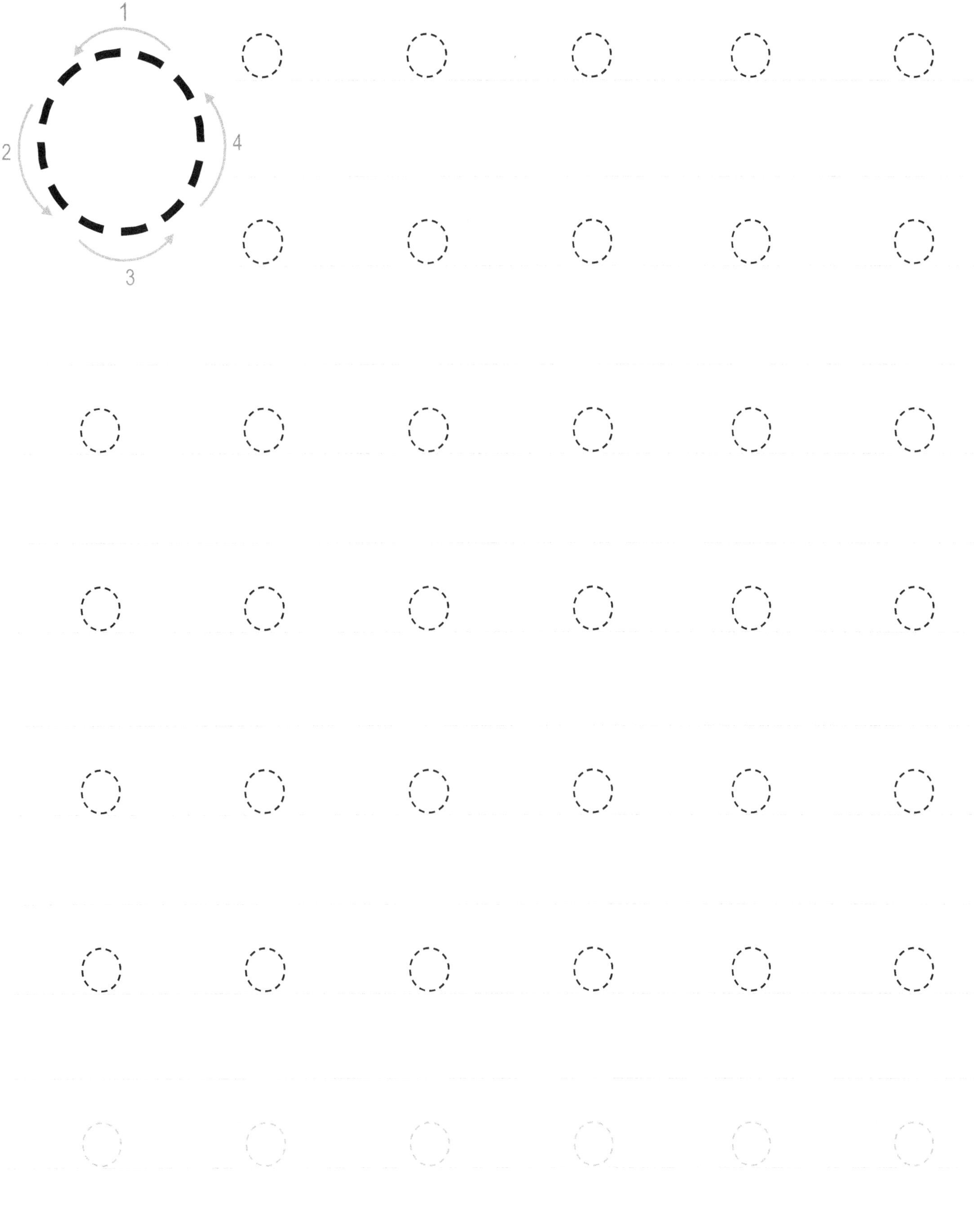
1
2
3
4

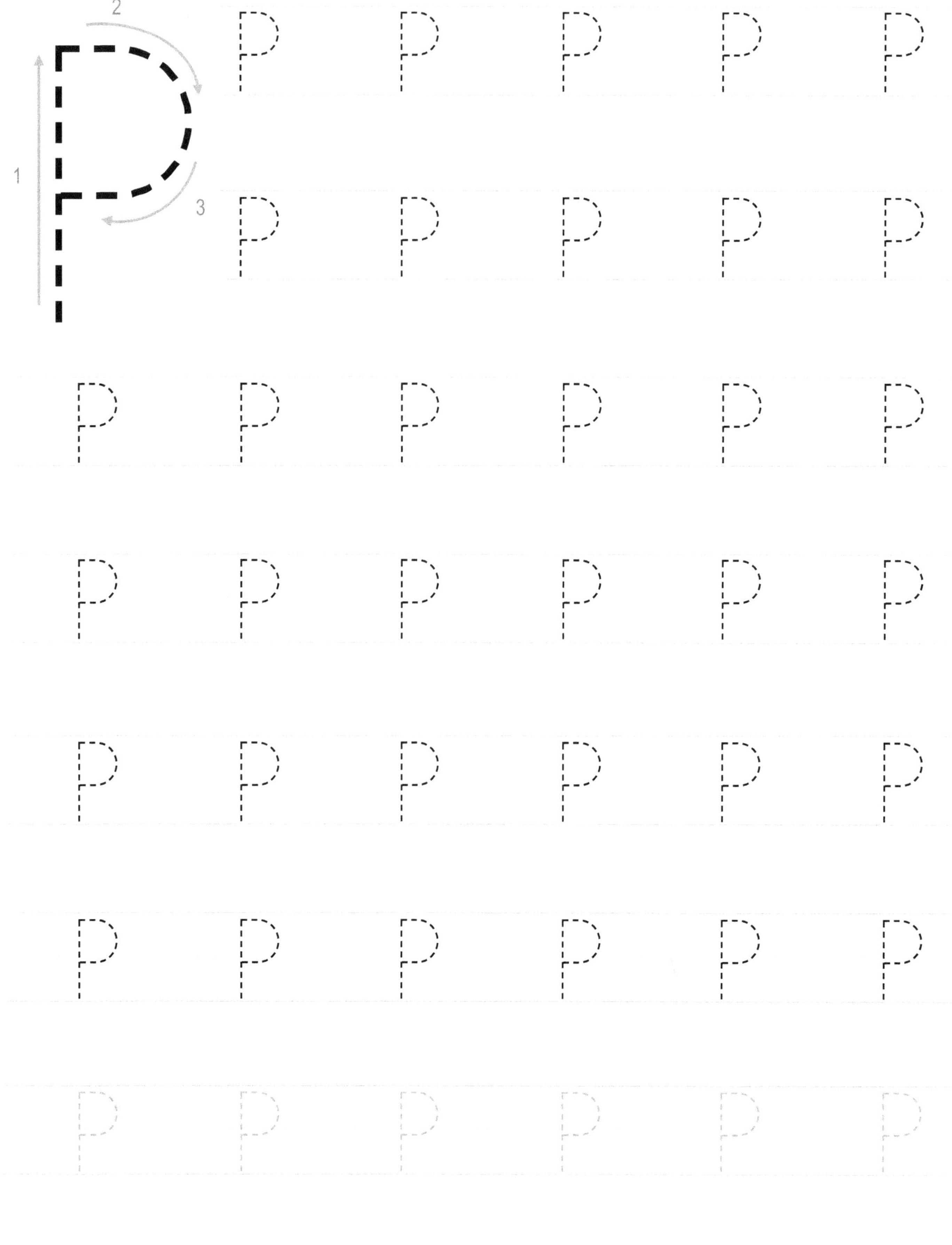
2
1
3

2

1 p 3

p p p p p

p p p p p

p p p p p p

p p p p p p

p p p p p p

p p p p p p

p p p p p p

1
2
3

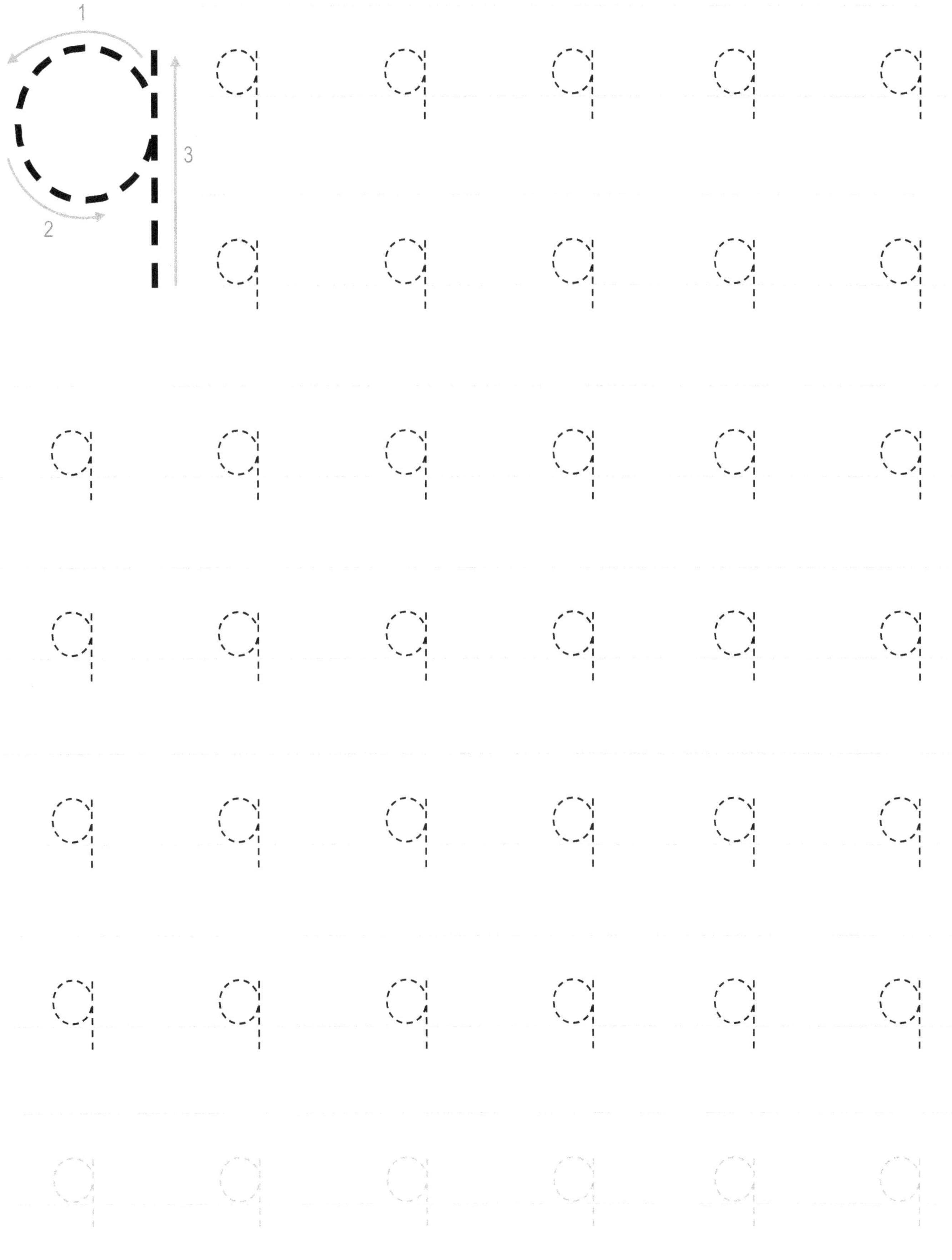
1
3
2

2

1 R 3 R R R R R

4 R R R R R

R R R R R R

R R R R R R

R R R R R R

R R R R R R

R R R R R R

1
2

1
2
3
4

1
2
3

1
2

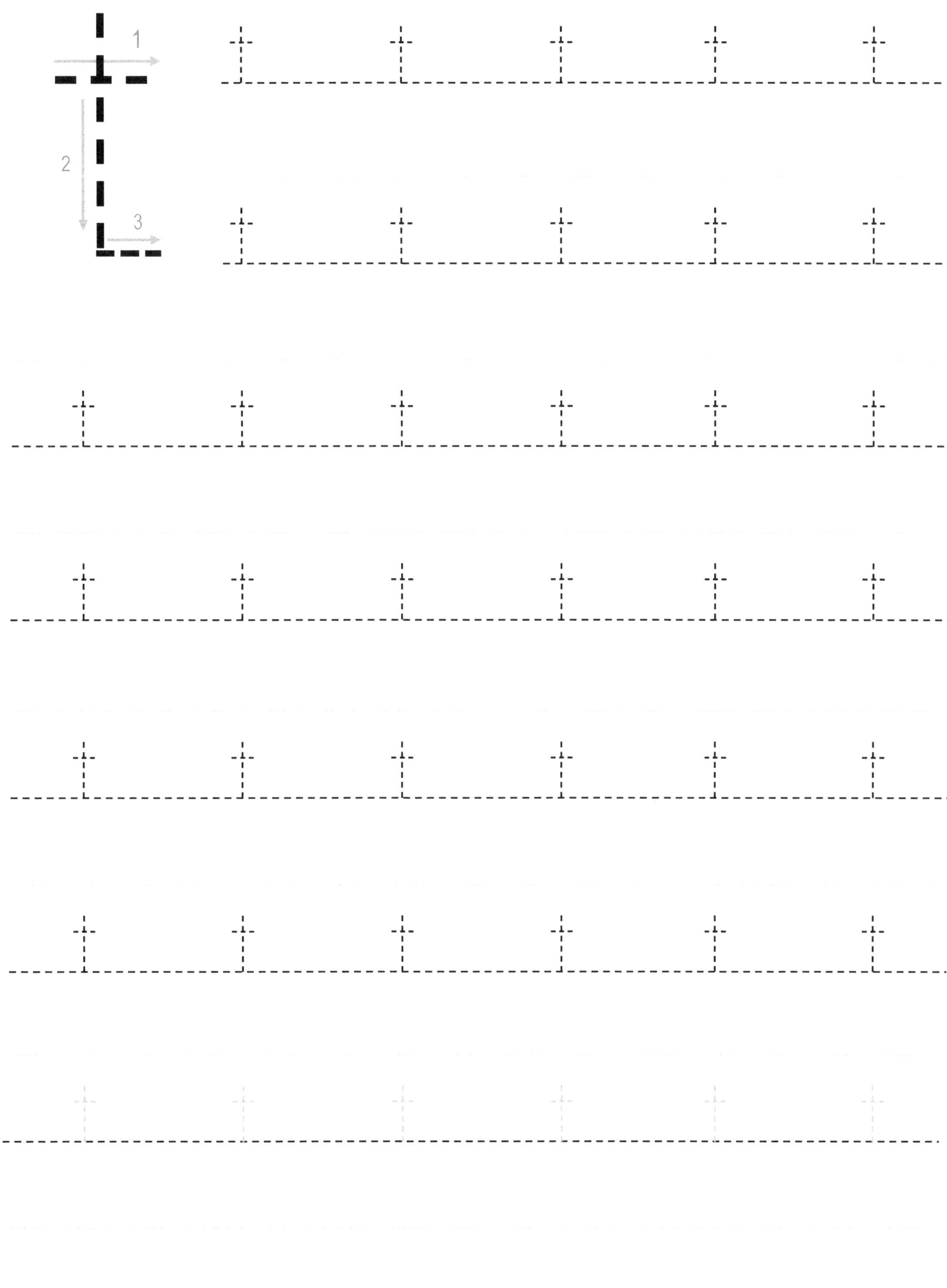

1
2
3

1
2
3

1
2
3

1
2

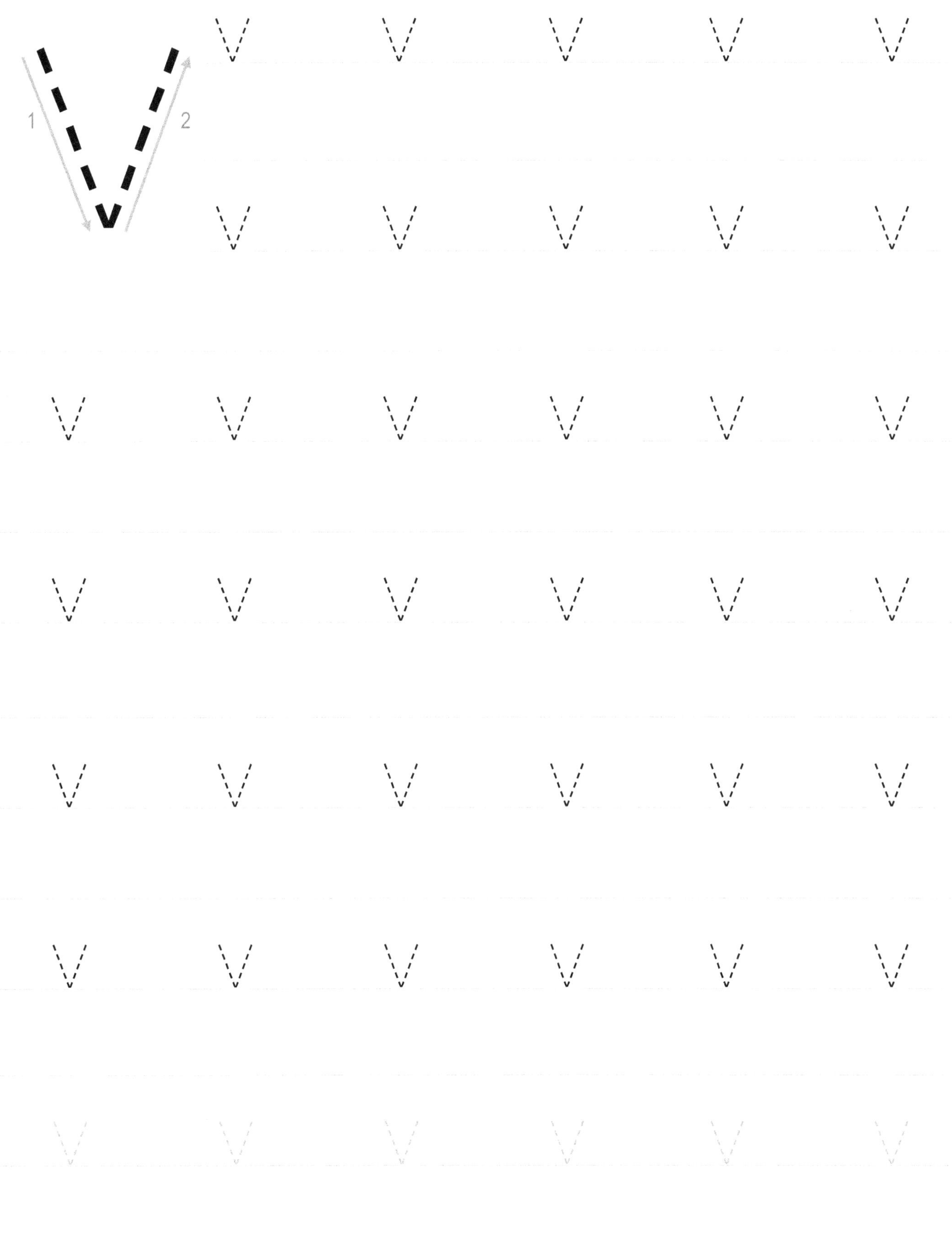

1
2

1
2
3
4

1
2
3
4

1
2

1
2

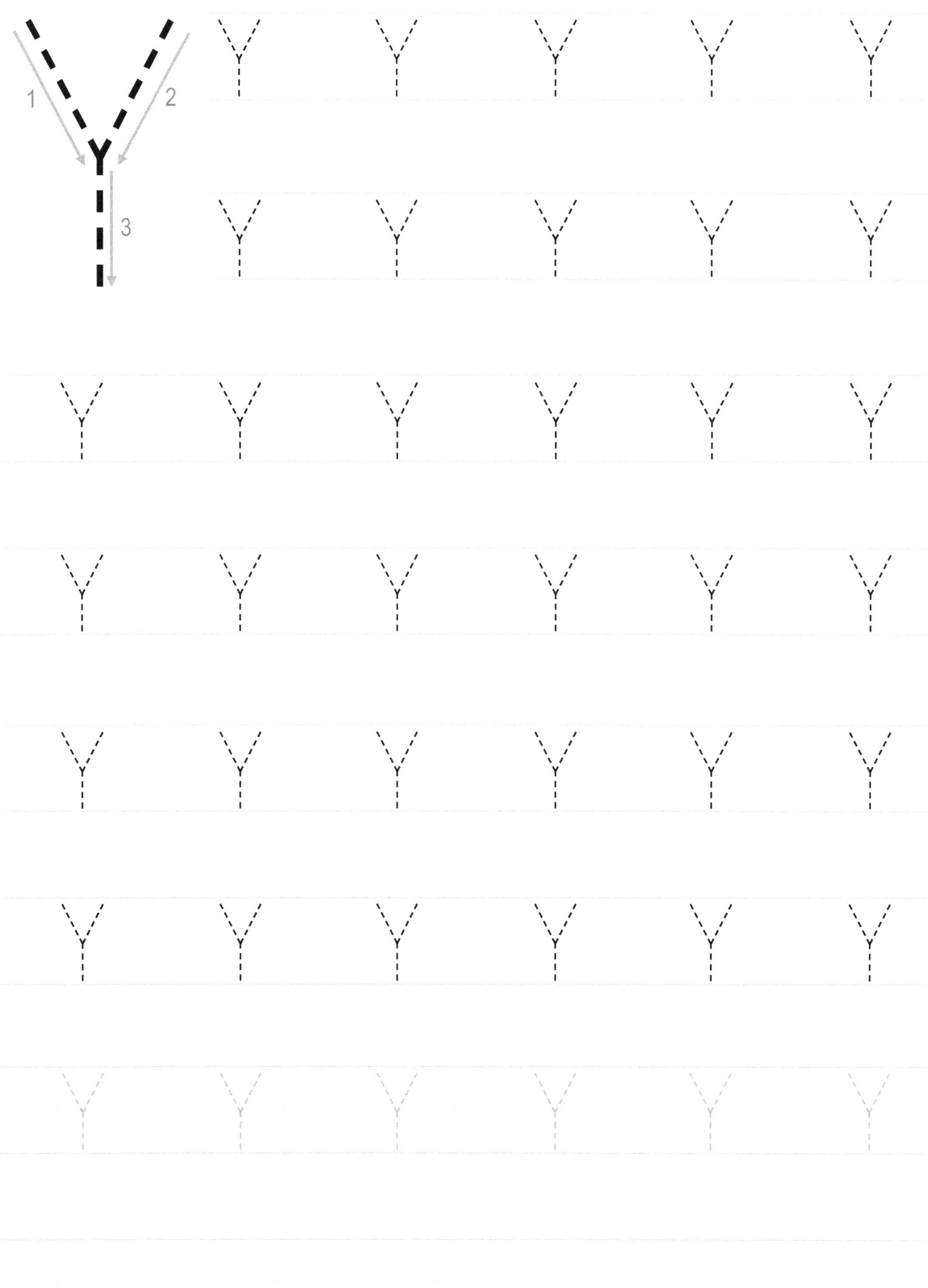
1
2
3

1
2

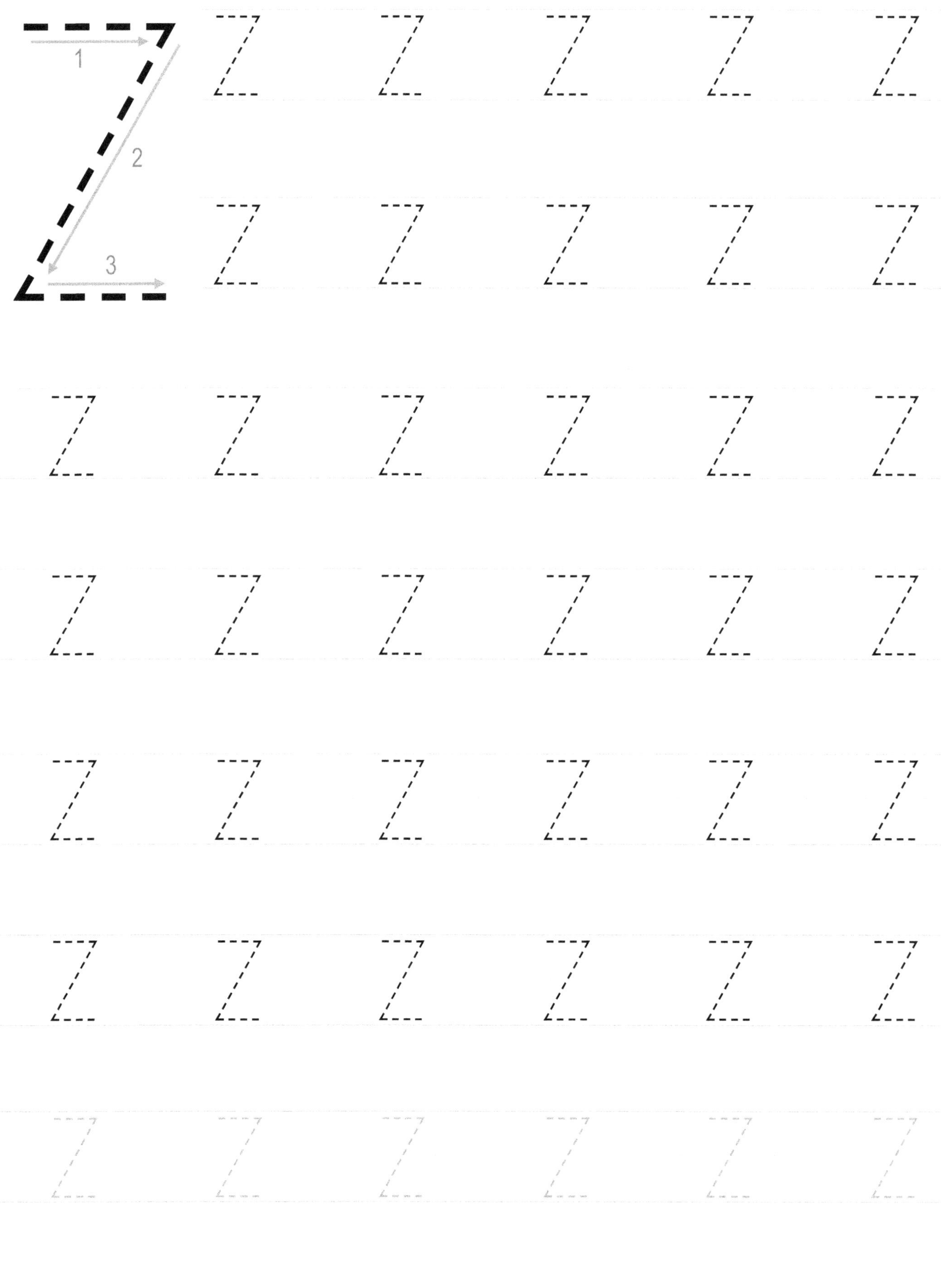
1
2
3

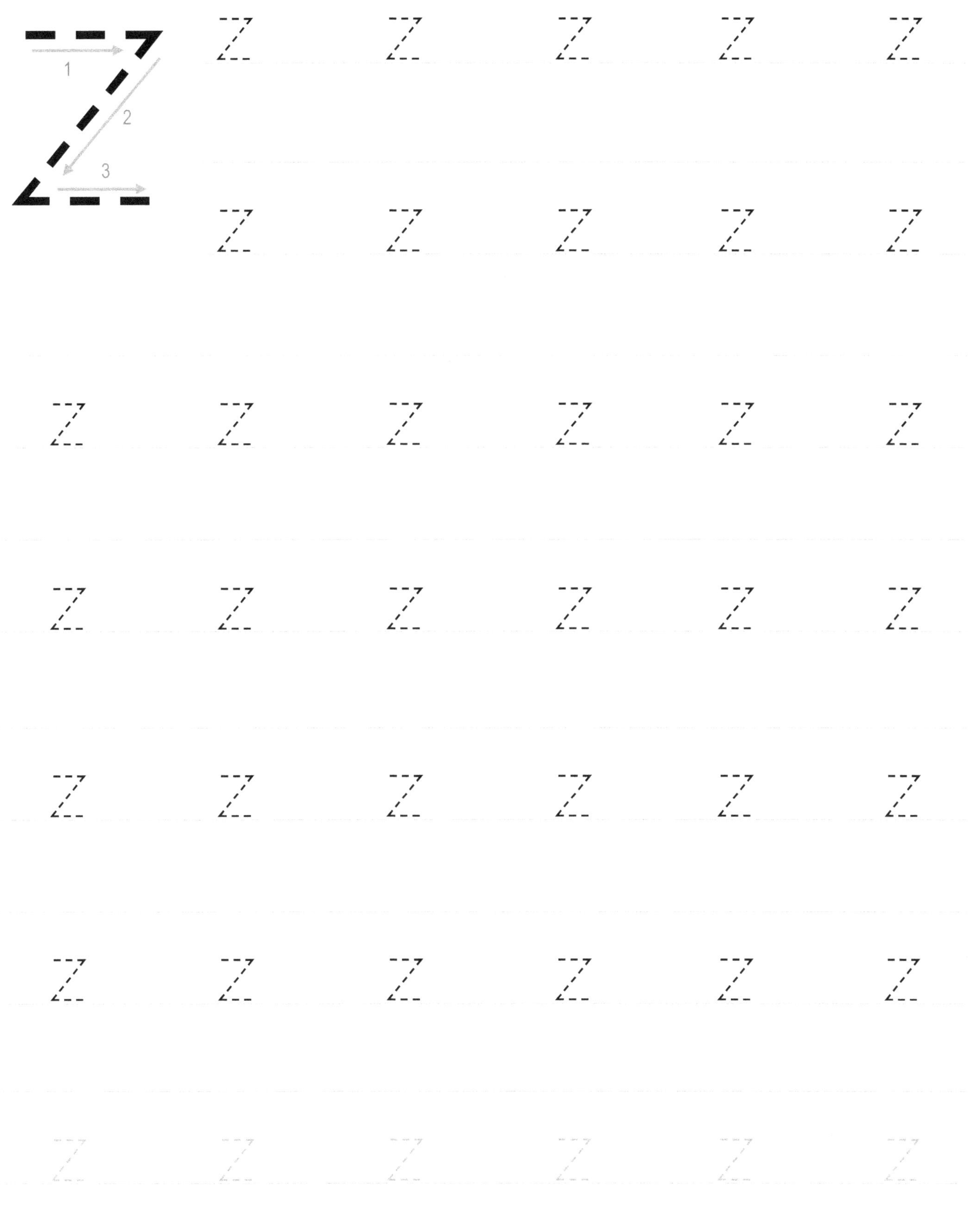
1
2
3

CERTIFICATE
of COMPLETION

Presented to

____

For ______________________________

______________ ______________

Date Signed

SCHOOL BUS

www.ingramcontent.com/pod-product-compliance
Lightning Source LLC
LaVergne TN
LVHW080555160826
845677LV00010B/1859
* 9 7 9 8 7 1 5 2 9 0 4 3 4 *